Free Agent

Free Agent

The Independent Professional's Roadmap to Self-Employment Success

Katy Tynan

CRC Press
Taylor & Francis Group
Boca Raton   London   New York

CRC Press is an imprint of the
Taylor & Francis Group, an **informa** business

A PRODUCTIVITY PRESS BOOK

CRC Press
Taylor & Francis Group
6000 Broken Sound Parkway NW, Suite 300
Boca Raton, FL 33487-2742

Printed on acid-free paper
Version Date: 20150105

International Standard Book Number-13: 978-1-4822-5881-3 (Paperback)

Library of Congress Cataloging-in-Publication Data

Tynan, Katy.
    Free agent : the independent professional's roadmap for self-employment success / Katy Tynan.
        pages cm
    Summary: "The full-time employee, the staple of the US workplace, is becoming an endangered species. We are on the brink of a seismic shift in the employer/employee relationship that will redefine the nature of jobs and careers. This book describes what's driving this change and includes a pragmatic action plan for professionals who wish to survive the challenge of how to be successful in this "new skills marketplace""-- Provided by publisher.
    Includes bibliographical references and index.
    ISBN 978-1-4822-5881-3 (paperback)
    1. Self-employed. 2. Professional employees. 3. Career development. I. Title.

HD8036.T96 2015
658.1'141--dc23   2014039865

Visit the Taylor & Francis Web site at
http://www.taylorandfrancis.com

and the CRC Press Web site at
http://www.crcpress.com

Contents

Introduction

Work is changing. Recent graduates, researchers who follow workforce trends, HR professionals, and entrepreneurs are buzzing about how the 9-to-5 job is dead, and how the smartest people are choosing to work independently rather than pursue traditional employment. Based on a recent survey, MBO Partners is predicting that by 2020 nearly half the workforce will be independent professionals who choose to sell their services to businesses as free agents. The Freelancers Union, a New York based benefits provider and advocacy organization, reports growth of more than 400% in its membership since launching in 2007. Gone are the days when freelancing was considered something people did between jobs.

While these numbers are driving headlines about the changing face of working professionals, the reality is that independent professionals have been a large percentage of the labor force for decades. Although surveys differ on how to count and classify the independent workforce, the IRS, the Bureau of Labor Statistics, and the U.S. Census all agree that freelance and self-employed workers account for a significant part of the economy, and have for decades. The last time the U.S. government officially counted the entire free agent workforce was in a 2006 survey by the GAO (Government Accountability Office), where they found that 42 million people, or just under one third of the total workforce, were doing some form of independent work.

Yet, despite the impact of this substantial demographic of workers on the economy, most people who are free agents for a living do so without formal training. They have never been taught how to run their own businesses, and they operate without the safety net of unemployment insurance, disability insurance, paid time off, or any of the other benefits that employees have. If you ask freelancers how they got started, most of them will tell you they had to figure it out for themselves, and many will admit to stress and anxiety about topics such as business structure, contracts, taxes, and insurance.

This support gap exists for a variety of reasons, not least of which is that our education system was designed to train people in the skills they needed to become productive employees, not free agents. In addition, where support exists in higher education or through services provided by the government, it exists to support small businesses and entrepreneurs, rather than people who simply want to work as an army of one.

It is true that being an employee comes (usually) with benefits and a structure that make it easy for people with jobs to pay their taxes and have access to benefits and a safety net. However, for many working professionals, a full-time job comes with drawbacks, too. Despite numerous high-profile efforts by companies to implement workplace flexibility programs, most businesses still require the average employee to adhere to a strict schedule, and to come into the office regularly rather than working from home or wherever they are most productive.

In fact, employee satisfaction numbers are at an all-time low, dipping below 50% in a recent survey by The Conference Board. Moreover, research experts at Gallup report that less than 30% of U.S. workers report being actively engaged with their work, leaving over 70% of the employees in the workforce to simply go through the motions and collect a paycheck.

It is no surprise if people find work so uninspiring that many are looking for alternatives. Elance, a freelance industry job board, found in its survey of freelancers that 70% were happier on their own than when they were working as employees, and 80% said they were more productive. An increasing number of professionals are choosing to opt out of working for an employer, both for the enjoyment of the work and the flexibility that being a free agent offers.

Along with this recent surge in the number of professionals (writers, web designers, business consultants, programmers, and photographers, just to name a few of the highest growth freelance roles), independent workers have seen a welcome increase in services and support for people who choose this career path. From organizations like The Freelancers Union, to co-working spaces, which offer a community and networking opportunity for independent professionals, a variety of tools and resources are emerging to support the needs of free agents. With cloud-based technology solutions that offer inexpensive storage, website solutions, email, and video conferencing, freelancers have access to all the tools they need to run their businesses from anywhere.

With a growing sense of community and support, the number of people considering free agency is growing by the day. However, despite the proliferation of people engaging in this work for all the benefits it offers, the path to success is still not always smooth. Working independently involves being responsible for things like withholding taxes, buying insurance, and keeping track of your own financials in ways you might not have had to do before.

In order to transition successfully from employee to free agent, you need to have a plan to avoid the pitfalls, and a support team to give you the expertise you need on complicated topics such as business structure, contracts, and accounting. There is an art and a science to developing great client relationships, pricing your services, and building your network.

This book is your guide to successfully navigating the transition. In the first few chapters, we will talk about how work is changing, and what is driving the growth of freelancing as a trend. In the second section, we will talk through the nitty gritty of how to get your new independent venture off the ground, how to find your first client, and what you need to know to stay out of trouble. Finally, in the last section we will talk about how to optimize your new freelance work style to make the most of your time and energy, so you can focus on doing more of what you love.

Becoming a free agent is about choosing to create the life that you want, creating revenue by doing work you enjoy on your own terms. Although it won't all be smooth sailing, with the right guidance and tools, you can make the switch to working for yourself. Eighty percent of freelancers say they are happier than when they were employees, so what are you waiting for?

Section I

The Emerging Trend of the Free Agent Labor Force

1

The Roots of Workplace Change

ZEELAND, Michigan—D.J. DePree was just 18 years old when he took his first shift as a clerk at the Star Furniture Company in 1909. He worked in the office filing, running errands, and making coffee. Over the next 15 years, DePree held every job in the growing firm and as his experience grew, so did his desire to be more than an employee. In 1923, he convinced his father-in-law to back him financially and DePree became the majority stakeholder in what was then the Michigan Star Furniture Company.

As the grip of the Great Depression tightened, the young executive recognized that the business model he had relied on for consistent sales over the last 30 years would not last much longer. Desperate for a way to stay afloat, he spent his days walking the floor of his now eerily quiet showroom in Grand Rapids. It was there that he struck up a relationship with a New York designer named Gilbert Rohde.

The mood in the marketplace and in boardrooms across the nation was grim. Just two years removed from the stock market crash of 1929, the once thriving firm teetered on the edge of bankruptcy. High-end bedroom suites handcrafted by skilled artisans were a luxury, and in the depths of the Great Depression, sales were abysmal. The leaders and stakeholders of the firm gathered to hear an announcement from their owner and they hoped it wasn't the end of the line for the enterprise. It was then that DePree unveiled a partnership with Rohde, and a plan that would lead them through the crisis. In the following months and years, the company shifted its focus from bedroom sets to manufacturing a line of practical office furnishings.

By the end of 1942, it began to sell what would become its landmark product—a light and versatile modular offering for office environments. D.J. DePree is not a household name, but you may be familiar with the name of his father-in-law, the man the company was named after: Herman

Miller. And if you've worked in an office anytime in the last 50 years, you've probably sat in the now infamous 1967 invention—the Action Office, also known as the cubicle. Between 1967 and today, Herman Miller emerged as the industry leader in creative furniture design for the modern workplace, capitalizing on a complete shift in the way businesses function.

Most of the factory floors of the turn-of-the century manufacturing economy are gone; today's products are designed, marketed, sold, and serviced by workers sitting in front of computers. Much of the actual production of goods is done overseas. The workforce of the twenty-first century sits in ergonomically correct chairs, with height-adjusted monitors, typing away on curved keyboards with gel wrist rests.

The cubicle is a pervasive symbol of the modern workplace. Nothing so clearly exemplifies the relationship between individuals and corporations as the beige enclosure with its horizontal counter space and modular storage drawers. Famously satirized by Scott Adam's *Dilbert*, the cubicle is as iconic to the modern workplace as the town saloon is to the western movie set. However, just 50 years ago it didn't exist.

Every business model and industry succeeds or fails based on its ability to adapt to change. D.J. DePree successfully navigated Herman Miller through the biggest financial crisis of his lifetime by moving with change rather than resisting it. Of course, change didn't stop with the end of the depression; in fact, if anything it has accelerated over the last 75 years. Ironically, as we look forward to try to guess how change will come to the workplace of tomorrow, research being released by that same innovative company is allowing us to see a glimpse of what the future holds. In October 2013, Herman Miller released the results of an extensive study of workplace trends, and will be basing their newest designs on these shifts in how people are working. These shifts give us insight into the future of working.

By 2015, the survey predicted an 83% increase in collaborative space and a 76%-decline in individual space. They also foresee a nearly 70%-increase in the number of employers who expect to provide work-at-home options. The inventor of the cubicle is predicting its obsolescence in just a few years. It is clear that the way we have been working for the last 20 years may not be the way we work over the next decade.

The shift to more flexible and more collaborative workspace is not just about providing different modalities of working for employees. A large part of this trend is the disaggregation of the professional workforce in general. The idea of a one-to-one relationship between individuals and employers has also shifted. Professionals with skills are finding that they get more value out of operating independently instead of being tied to a single company. These smart professionals have transitioned to a one-to-many relationship through building a portfolio of clients instead of having a single employer.

We see independent working as a growing trend—we read articles about the growth and change that is happening in the United States and around the world, but why is it taking place? What is driving these changes in how people relate to companies? To answer these questions, we need to look back at the last major workplace change and at a few other key factors that are at the root of these trends and transitions.

THE DRIVERS OF CHANGE

As part of the Revenue Act of 1978, the United States Congress passed a little known provision designed to limit the perks of highly paid executives. That legislative footnote unexpectedly and unintentionally changed the fundamental nature of how employers and employees relate to one another. It contributed to a massive shift from 20+ year careers with one company to today's average 3- to 5-year tenure. It is at the heart of the debate about social security and retirement, and it is why most companies spend more on recruiting today than they do on employee development.

Today we know that provision as IRS section 401(k). It is the regulation that allowed for a new type of tax deferred savings plan that caught on like wildfire and became the most prevalent retirement vehicle offered by employers in the United States. Between 1980 and 2012, the percentage of Fortune 100 companies offering fixed benefit pension plans plummeted from over 90% to less than 10% as the 401(k) soared into widespread adoption.

How did something as simple as a retirement plan change the fundamental nature of the relationship between individuals and their employers? Simple—portability. By shedding the responsibility of managing pension plans, employers put retirement savings directly into the hands of employees, freeing them from one of the major downsides of changing jobs. In the days of pensions, the longer you worked at a company, the bigger your pension would be at retirement.

The pension system was built to encourage employee loyalty. However, with the shift to the 401(k) and the ability to take their retirement savings with them, employees found that changing jobs for better money and more career opportunity was greatly to their advantage. It would no longer hurt their chances for a stable retirement, and opened the door to more money and more interesting work along the way.

Over the last 30 years, the average tenure of employees has dropped from 20 years to less than 5. It continues to decline, as the Millennial generation enters the workforce with expectations of changing employers every 1 to 3 years.* Savvy employees have become active free agents who are always on the lookout for new opportunities. Employers have taken to hiring ideal candidates with the skills they need from outside the company as opposed to investing time and money developing internal candidates who might take those skills and go elsewhere with them. By the turn of the twenty-first century, the 40-year career and the three-pronged retirement plan (pension + Social Security + savings) had gone the way of the dodo bird.

While the 401(k) regulation was not the only factor that contributed to the shift away from long careers with one employer, it was without a doubt one of the snowflakes that ultimately led to an avalanche of change in how the workplace works. It is a great example that nothing about our working world is set in stone. Looking at the past, it is easy to see how the workplace has adapted. So let us now turn to the future and look at some of the factors in play today that will shape the workplace of our future.

Factor 1—The Great Recession

In 2007, the U.S. economy was teetering on the brink of disaster. Decades of questionable practices in the mortgage investment marketplace had created a bubble in the housing market. As investment banks started losing money on defaulting loans, a ripple effect plunged larger banks and insurance companies into a spiral of losses. The housing bubble burst and the U.S. economy began its steep slide into recession.

Because of the terrible economy, many people were pushed abruptly into part-time work or self-employment. Some were the victims of layoffs and downsizing initiatives; others saw their employers go out of business and disappear right underneath them.

In response to market pressures to cut costs just to stay solvent, many companies made a decision to transition as much work as possible to contractors, believing that this system would make them more resilient. If they had more work to do, they could bring on more contractors or ramp up

---

* *Source*: Millennial Compass Report by MLS Group and Ashbridge Business School.

the number of hours that their existing consultants were working. If they needed to cut costs, they could easily reduce hours and slow non-essential projects. The contractor strategy meant they could stay away from layoffs and the expensive hassle of ramping down salaried employees.

The strategy worked. In fact, it worked so well that when the economy began to recover, many organizations opted to keep leveraging the contingent work force in the form of contractors and freelancers instead of hiring back full-time employees. While this concept saved many companies from going under, it left hundreds of thousands of Americans facing an unplanned career shift out of the traditional full-time, salaried workforce.

Factor 2—Employer to Enemy

If the rise of the 401(k) created a loyalty gap between people and their employers, the Great Recession widened that gap into a chasm. Relentless news coverage of corporate executives laying off hundreds of workers and cutting benefits while riding home on their private jets to their lavish family compounds deepened a growing sense that companies were profiting unfairly on the backs of the middle class.

As employers became increasingly vilified either as the cause of the recession (banks and investors) or as the face of layoffs and downsizing initiatives, an entrenched feeling of self-preservation emerged among the average American. No longer bound to their employer through a pension plan and resentful of job cuts and a never-ending trend of "do more with less," many individuals began to strongly consider whether they would be better off taking their chances with self-employment.

But one benefit remained difficult to obtain without a full-time job. Health insurance was still a strong tie binding employees to their companies.

Factor 3—The Patient Protection and Affordable Care Act (PPACA)

For over three decades, the cost of health care has been rising exponentially, both because premiums have risen and because employers have cut back on the percentage of the cost of insurance that they are subsidizing.

Under the administration of President Bill Clinton in the 1990s, the federal government tried and failed to implement universal health care. By the 2008 election cycle, it was one of the most important planks in Barack

Obama's election platform. In 2010, just two years into his first term, he signed the Affordable Care Act into law.

For the next two years, a series of legal challenges threatened the newly passed law, and the country waited and watched to see whether the legislation would hold up in court. On June 28, 2012, the wait ended with the Supreme Court voting 5–4 that Congress had not acted outside of its authority by levying this tax. Over the next two years, the implementation rolled forward toward full adoption.

While the revenue act that launched the 401(k) went largely unnoticed by the working public in 1978, the Affordable Care Act has been at the center of a highly public and contentious national debate about the role of government. Both parties, as well as private interests, have spent untold amounts of money attempting to educate the American public about the potential benefits and drawbacks to this initiative. However, no matter which side you are on, there is no doubt that this law will have an enormous impact on the relationship between people and companies.

Having universal access to health insurance that no longer relies on full-time employment will eliminate one of the last significant supports underpinning the full-time employment construct. As that structure crumbles, new ways of working are emerging and becoming the rule rather than the exception.

These three factors—the Great Recession, the change in how people perceive their relationship with their employers, and the rollout of the Affordable Care Act—are the most significant drivers of changes in how the workplace works. However, there are other factors related to this change, too, and in a sense, they are responsible for some of the more positive aspects of this transition.

Generational Factors

Each generation of workers deals with the working world a little differently. While the children of the depression and the post-war economy had a strong bond with their employers, over time that relationship has become weaker. Therefore, as change comes to the workplace, each generation's vision of what "work" looks like is changing as well.

As the Baby Boomer generation approaches retirement, many of its members want to stay busy and, particularly, want to continue to earn some income while pursuing something that matters. Having built up strong career portfolios, the Boomers are in a great position to transition to consulting. It is flexible, it often pays well, and it allows them to continue to work and stay engaged on their own terms.

Coming just behind the Baby Boomers are the children of Generation X. At the midpoint of their careers, this demographic ranges from about 30 to 45 years old. Skeptical about employers and the likelihood of entitlements like Social Security being solvent when they reach retirement, some members of GenX have been early adopters of the flexible workplace. They are also the most likely group to have been laid off during the recession because they are the higher paid middle managers who were not close enough to retirement to take an early option.

The youngest members of the workforce, Generation Y or the Millennials, are the most likely to experience these changes throughout the whole scope of their careers. Despite their uncertainty, the Millennials may be the best positioned to take advantage of this change because they do not have years of entrenched ideas of what job stability looks like.

A CASE STUDY OF THE NEW MODEL

As the economy shifts to a hybrid of working people with "normal" jobs mixed with an increasing percentage of free agents who work when and where they can, a new type of career path is emerging. In his 2007 blockbuster *The Four-Hour Workweek*, Tim Ferris argued that if you want to be wealthy and control your own destiny, a job is not the way to do that. He was not the first or the last to make such an argument, but the practical process of achieving that goal still eludes many working people.

In writing this book, I talked to a wide variety of people whose work is well along the path to this new self-directed and self-managed way of working. They come from all walks of life and have found a way to leverage their own initiative to create a work–life blend that makes sense. In the subsequent chapters, we will meet many more of these smart, talented people and deconstruct how they made the leap successfully. For now, let's look briefly at the example of social media pioneer Chris Brogan.

For 16 years, Chris had a regular job in the telecommunications industry. As he describes it, this meant he spent 1 hour working and 7 hours finding ways to fill his time so he could look busy and keep getting paid. Chris says, "I could get my entire day job done in about 48 minutes on most days, leaving me with hours of free time and no one really caring much about what I did."

This is one of the mismatches between old ways of working and new ones. Not every job is optimized for a 40-hour, Monday to Friday work-week. However, most companies still expect workers to fit into this framework. Chris spent much of his early career working in a very traditionally structured position, and because he had been brought up to think that a 9-to-5 stable job was the definition of success, he thought he was happy.

One day at an industry event he ran into a friend who talked him into joining up with him in a new initiative called PodCamp. PodCamp launched in 2006 as a series of community building events in the early days of social media, and grew out of the popularity of iPod "podcasts." When Chris landed the PodCamp gig, he realized how different it felt to pursue a passion as opposed to doing a job.

"I had lots of roles from software deployment engineering to project management," Chris says, "I loved all of it, but when I ran off to join the circus and run events and the like, I knew that I'd found my calling. I love the business of media and education." This is the blessing of stepping outside of the standard working world box. You have the opportunity to do work you truly enjoy, and to focus on those aspects of your work that are most meaningful to you.

But with that opportunity comes the responsibility of managing a lot of things that more conventional jobs have always managed for you. Once you are on your own, you are responsible for things like self-employment tax, getting new clients, and ensuring you are paid for your work. For many people these are daunting hurdles, but the structural changes in the working world mean that tackling them is easier than it used to be—and for people like Chris, the benefits of doing so are substantial.

Making the transition from the corporate world to becoming an independent operator does not in any sense mean that Chris has stopped working or stopped earning income. In fact, it is the challenge of being successful, of generating revenue, and of helping others do the same that drives him to focus on his endeavors these days. He loves the flexibility that this model brings both to his own work and to the people with whom he works.

"I love that it's built around effectiveness, and that my team can work wherever there's Wi-Fi. I love that I'm able to work closely with professionals who want to work the way they want to work, only better, and that my courses and material reach deeper than my speeches used to manage. I love that I'm responsible for my revenue. I love that I have the challenge of feeding all the mouths and figuring out how to earn even more so that we can try and grow in some of the painful ways that very small companies must grow."

Having all of these advantages and responsibilities, though, means that Chris's current working processes are radically different from how he operated in the corporate world. In fact, he says they are different, at least in part, because of the lessons he learned being part of that ecosystem. He "feels that most corporate structures work in spite of themselves, not because they're great ideas," and says that one of the reasons for his success is that he has focused on the people—the human factor that drives so many aspects of business and leadership.

Increasingly, the new generation of workers says it is interested in launching flexible careers that incorporate consulting and self-employment. A 2011 study by oDesk found that 61% percent of respondents with full time, salaried jobs said they would likely quit those jobs within two years to shift to flexible alternatives such as contracting or consulting. Raised in the Internet era and a period of shifting work requirements and expectations, these workers are skilled at building strong networks through social media and leveraging technology to share ideas. Once they get some experience under their belts, they will be powerful competitors in this new marketplace.

Throughout this chapter, we have been looking at the past and considering the present in order to try to predict what is next. While theory is a good and important place to start, much of the rest of this book will be a practical roadmap for your success. The goal of understanding change is to be ahead of it—to take action today so that when the shifts in career management come, you will be ready. In the next chapter, we take a deep dive into the demographics of the free agent trend. We will look at some of the confusing statistics and see why they sometimes seem to point in opposite directions. We will look at what professions are growing and which are shrinking, and we will start to understand where the best opportunities exist to make a great living as a free agent.

2

How We Got Here

Consuming millions of gallons of gasoline and nearly as many hours of time, employees of companies large and small make the daily pilgrimage from their homes to workplaces. Seventy percent of working Americans have full-time jobs, making roughly 120 million people participating in the daily grind of getting to work each day.

For a majority of Americans, the 40-hour workweek is a familiar and entrenched construct, which represents how we make the money that pays the bills and allows us to have things like houses and cars and flat-screen TVs. It is what we know and how we are taught to make a living by our parents and our education system. While there is a lot of conversation around the growth of freelancing as a modern trend that is booming due to technology, the reality is that people have been working for themselves for most of history.

For hundreds of years prior to our modern concept of employers and commuting, most people lived and worked on farms. There were no factories, no industrial production, and where there were services, they were services for farmers. The term "gentleman farmer" and "prosperous farmer" applied equally to those making a good living and generating a comfortable standard of living from working the land.

But that all changed in the nineteenth century when the industrial revolution fundamentally altered the way people lived and worked. Factories were born. People needed to learn new skills in order to be successful. New job functions like "foreman" and "manager" sprang into the business lexicon. As industries grew and became concentrated in and around urban centers, people began to do something new. They had to travel to get to work.

Commute, from the Latin "*mutar*" meaning to change, is the word we use to describe the daily trek people make to and from work. In the morning, they make the transition from their homes to their jobs, and then in the evening they migrate back again. It is the physical manifestation of the idea that work and home are two separate ecosystems.

In the farming economy, there was no physical difference between your work and your home, but by the early twentieth century, most Americans had become accustomed to a separation of these two environments. In fact, it was common practice to keep your personal life completely out of your work and not even to discuss family or home issues in the workplace.

In the late twentieth century, advances in technology began to revolutionize the way people communicated, interacted, and how and where they could work. The physical separation of work and home still existed, but technology allowed employees to be accessible and to connect with the office in both places. In just a few short years, these new communication tools rejoined work with home, creating a substantial shift in how and where people worked.

For many, holding down a 40-hour per week job really means working 50 or more hours. Employers are demanding more, and commuting takes time too. Very few companies will allow you to be a parent in the office, so a full-time job means child care if you have kids. Buying into this system requires a delicate balance of workplace performance, functional childcare, and a working car.

In 2014, Bright Horizons commissioned the Modern Family Index—a survey that explores what it means to balance family and professional life. Their goal was to gain a better understanding of the reality of life as a working parent, including all of the challenges and struggles that entails. With advances in technology that allow most professionals to work from anywhere, and an increasing body of research showing that flexibility is an important component of employee satisfaction, you might expect that this survey would show that today's modern family blends home and work in a seamless way.

You would be wrong.

Eighty percent of modern families have two working parents in the home, and the challenge of juggling the needs of home and family with the needs of employers is top of mind for most parents. An astounding 48% of those interviewed for the study reported being afraid that responding to the needs of their family would get them fired if it conflicted with their ability to deliver on their responsibilities on the job.

Clearly, the relationship between work and home is not as smooth as it might be. Furthermore, an increasing number of fathers (43% versus 52%

of mothers) reported a high level of stress related to balancing their kids' needs with the needs of their bosses.

How can this be? The new millennium was supposed to be the era of the mobile work force where everyone broke free of the chains of the office and had the opportunity to balance work and life. Despite a substantial body of research that shows flexible working programs increase productivity, improve retention, and have a high correlation to employee engagement, we have seen a swath of large, influential companies cutting back or eliminating flexibility within their work environments.

In 2005, Bank of America launched a broad-based telecommuting initiative, touting it as a driver of employee productivity and satisfaction. Despite its popularity, at the tail end of 2012 it was reviewed and substantially curtailed. This was the first in a series of high-profile companies ending or severely limiting their workplace flexibility programs. In February 2013, Yahoo's new CEO Marissa Meyer presided over the termination of all remote work arrangements in the organization, and told employees they must either report to a Yahoo office or lose their jobs. Just a few months later, Best Buy eliminated its highly touted ROWE (Results Only Work Environment) program, which was based on the idea that when and where an individual worked was less important than what they produced.

While many organizations continue to claim a strong commitment to work–life balance and flexibility, the reality is that these arrangements are not nearly as accessible or as well supported as the recruiting materials claim, the main difference being the gap between flexibility options that are available versus those that are actually usable. In his study for the Sloan Center on Aging and Work at Boston College, Professor Stephen Sweet observed that while 78% of companies offered the option of reduced hours, fewer than 16% of companies offered that perk to a majority of their employees. In other words, the benefit was on the books for PR, but was not actually available to the average worker. In addition, while 94% of employers offered some level of ability to work remotely, that choice was not offered to all employees, but rather to a small subset.

Internally, large corporations were finding that managing flexibility programs required more overhead and more management than falling back to traditional schedules. However, one of the surprising outcomes of this decision was a shift toward employing an increasing number of contractors. Rather than having to manage flexibility programs in-house, corporations were finding that it was easier and more efficient to leverage the freelance labor pool. In addition, it happened that because of several years of a poor economy, that labor pool was extremely robust.

In 2007, when the housing bubble burst and the U.S. economy began its steep slide into recession, many people had their balanced lives disrupted as employers shed jobs in a desperate attempt to keep their businesses afloat. Some of those who went through this breakdown of the status quo were the victims of layoffs and downsizing initiatives, others saw their employers go out of business, and still others were stuck in a spiraling debt cycle with an underwater mortgage and more credit card debt than they could afford. In response to market pressures to cut costs just to stay solvent, employers increasingly transitioned work to contractors, believing that this system would make their companies more resilient. If they had more work to do, they could bring on more contractors or ramp up the number of hours that their existing consultants were working, but they were not tied into the costs and inflexibility of full-time employees.

Jeff Wald is one of the founders of Work Market—a company that helps big businesses leverage what he refers to as the contingent workforce. As someone who spends all of his time facilitating the relationship between companies and contract workers, he is very close to the process and has some great insights on how people and companies relate to each other outside of the typical employer/employee model.

Traditionally, when the economy is great, the number of freelancers and free agents drops. Jobs are plentiful, unemployment is low, and most people choose a job over a freelance career. When the economy is bad, employers cut jobs, and we generally see an increase in the number of contractors, consultants, and other independent workers. However, Jeff and his partners have observed a shift in this pattern in recent years. Despite the improving economy, the number of independent professionals has increased. Work Market's growth is a testament to this decoupling of the relationship between the state of the economy and the number of people freelancing.

Work Market is Jeff's third startup, so he is no stranger to employment, self-employment, and how businesses operate. Like many successful entrepreneurs, Jeff is an observer. He watches the process of business, the way that companies work, and the things with which they struggle. The very best opportunity for a successful venture is one where a specific type of organization has a problem that keeps it from doing something it wants to do. In this case, the problem that Jeff and his partners saw was how big companies engage with individual people outside of the boundaries of traditional employment.

In Chapter 1, we talked about the recovery from the great recession and how companies saw a big advantage in the flexibility of working with independent professionals. Full-time employees come with administrative overhead. You have to manage them, find places for them to sit, give them benefits, and pay a portion of their employment tax. However, contract labor can be much more flexible—workers can be engaged to pick up specific tasks and need to be paid only for the time they work. Smaller companies were taking advantage of this nimble, cost-effective workforce but bigger companies were not. They had a problem.

For Jeff, that problem was a great opportunity. By creating a structure that allowed large companies to engage with the contingent workforce, Work Market became a key player in the evolving landscape of the labor market. It is important to understand that big companies often do things for very different reasons and in very different ways than small companies do. Because of the scale of their operations, they cannot afford to assume that an unlikely thing will not happen. If you have 10 employees, an event that happens one time in a thousand is not very likely to happen to anyone at your firm. If you have 10,000 employees, it is likely to happen to approximately 10 of them.

Further, beyond the simple issue of scale, large companies are often more heavily regulated than small ones. Most of the provisions of the Affordable Care Act only apply (as of right now) to companies with over 50 full-time employees. Therefore, big companies have to spend more time and resources on understanding and complying with these new regulations. The reason Work Market is appealing to large companies is that they get all the benefits of working with a flexible workforce, while reducing some of the paperwork and the risk.

With organizations like Work Market coming to fill the gap and allow large corporations to leverage the power of independent professionals, and smaller organizations finding freelancers easier and more efficient to work with, the number of free agents in the workplace continues to grow.

While the official statistics say this particular recession is largely behind us, many companies saw the value of a more flexible, work-on-demand workforce, and so rather than shifting back toward hiring full-time employees again, they have maintained their policies of shifting work to contractors, consultants, and other part-time employees. Therefore, the recovery has not been the return to "normal" that many of us expected.

In addition, as we discussed in the last chapter, the capability of individuals to buy health insurance on their own has made it easier for people who want a DIY career and life. Not having to rely on an employer for such a basic need allows more people to separate their need for income from the requirement to work a rigid 40-hour schedule. As independent professionals become more the norm than the exception, the opportunities to negotiate flexible work schedules with employers get better and better.

One of the challenges of the 40-hour workweek is the idea that people are not like machines. Machines work at a steady pace during a set period of time, and produce consistent results throughout. Human physiology does not support this idea at all. In fact, the human body operates on a cycle that has an enormous impact on our ability to focus and work in a productive way. In 1953, Nathaniel Kleitman was studying sleep patterns. He was the first to observe and document the presence of REM—a period of deep sleep characterized by rapid eye movements.

He also observed (although this is less well publicized) that people continue that cycle during the day. Peretz Lavie observed the same phenomenon in 1981 and described it as "Ultradian Rhythm"—90-minute cycles of concentration separated by 15- to 20-minute rest breaks that allow for maximum productivity in the morning. The afternoon and evening hours are a little different, consisting of longer but less focused alert periods followed by natural tendencies to rest around 4:30 p.m. and 11:30 p.m.

If the modern workplace was adapted to leverage these cycles, productivity might soar, but for most, managers expect everyone to appear productive all day long, and working schedules are based around four hours of work (with a 15-minute break) followed by a 30-minute lunch, followed by four more hours of work.

The result of this combination of commuting, operating in an unnatural and artificial social structure, and attempting to over-ride our natural body rhythms is that many people feel stressed, anxious, and unhappy doing the work that takes up a large percentage of their day. The natural inclination of course is to go in the opposite direction and avoid work entirely.

While it is a nice thing to do for a few weeks, you would actually be just as unhappy doing nothing as you are working every day. The human brain needs stimulation—your body is designed to move and to be used.

Susan Cain, in her book *Quiet: The Power of Introverts in a World that Can't Stop Talking*, champions the idea that people have varying preferences for stimulation, and that we all have a "sweet spot"—an ideal balance between active, challenging work and rest/recovery. While the 8- to 10-hour workday might be the sweet spot for some, for many it is either far too much (stressed out, burned out) or far too little (bored, frustrated).

The reason Timothy Ferris can call his book *The Four-Hour Workweek* when his average day includes over 12 hours of activity, either physical or mental, is because he only considers something "work" if it is unpleasant. Most freelancers are putting in just as many hours (often more) as people working traditional jobs. It is just that they are choosing how to spend their time and what to prioritize, and they are allowing themselves to set a schedule that works for their own sweet spot of mental stimulation and accommodating the natural rhythms of their own bodies.

Most of us learned how to approach work by watching and listening to our parents. Unfortunately, the skills they taught us and the habits that worked for them are 20 years out of date (sometimes more if they practiced what they learned from their parents). Moreover, the pace of change in the workplace continues to accelerate so trying to do it the old way is increasingly becoming career-limiting behavior instead.

However, our parents are no longer our only options for role models. In the new world of global interconnectivity, we can look to a variety of people who have changed from this traditional model, and learn how to approach work in a different way. Steve Anderson, founder of a Boston-based consulting firm, described his happiest and most productive period when he was just launching the business out of his home.

> I lived and worked in a small loft apartment in the attic of a house. My bed was on one side of the room and my desk was on the other. I would wake up in the morning, roll out of bed, and work for a few hours. When I started to feel my energy run low, I would take a shower, walk down to the coffee shop for breakfast, and then head back up to my room. I'd work some more and then go out for a run or take a nap. It was a strange way of working but I felt more productive than I have at any other point in my career. I got so much done just working away without distraction and then taking breaks to work out or visit friends or talk to potential clients.

The industrial revolution brought about great change in the way people live and work. Technology has brought about a similar revolution over the last 20 years. We have shifted from blending life and work to separating them, and have come back now to a blend. In a sense, the employment marketplace is like the real estate market—it has cycles of supply and demand. When there are more houses than there are buyers, prices go down and sellers become motivated to be more flexible in the terms of sales. Historically, when there were more people out of work than there were jobs, the employers had the ability to define the terms of employment. However, as the market shifts and more professionals choose to work independently, employers are finding that they need to be more flexible to attract the talent they need.

Section II

How to Get Started

3

Making the Transition from Employee to Free Agent

It is 8 a.m. and light rain is falling outside the floor-to-ceiling glass windows of Foley Hoag—a prestigious law firm located in Boston's innovation district. One by one, people are trickling into the large conference room on the 12th floor. Coffee and a continental breakfast are laid out on the back wall, and eight large round tables are arranged around the room. At the front, alternately tapping away on his Smartphone and leaping up enthusiastically to greet newcomers, is our host. In jeans and a polo shirt, with shaggy hair and a sense of barely contained energy, he is the living stereotype of a tech entrepreneur. Distracted, casual, friendly, and clearly running in many directions, this is the man we have all paid to see.

This man is wealthy because he learned to make money from his unique talents. His name is Peter Shankman.

In 2008 in his apartment in New York, Shankman came up with a solution to a problem that had bothered him when he was working in AOL's newsroom in the early days of his career—how to rapidly identify sources for a news article. Shankman was well aware of the challenges that reporters on tight deadlines face when trying to find experts. With social media booming, he came up with an idea to leverage the 24/7 availability of resources like Twitter to allow reporters to reach out to millions of potential subject matter experts and find the right people to interview. His idea was a hit, and less than two years after founding it, the project was sold to marketing and PR firm Vocus.

Peter Shankman continues to churn out successful projects and ideas, primarily because he understands the idea of adding value.

Don't suck.

Find a way to help.

Like Chris Brogan, who we talked about in Chapter 1, Peter Shankman is successful because he recognized how he could use his unique talents to help a population of people solve a problem. At the core, this is the goal of all independent professionals. If you want to develop a steady stream of income, you have to be able to find a consistent way in which your talent creates value for someone else.

Value is not a new idea. Long before currency, work was valued through barter in the form of goods. Many years ago, we hosted a French exchange student in our home. He was fascinated by idioms—those unique expressions that don't always translate literally. One day he came home and asked us what the phrase "there's no free lunch" means. For an individual seeking to find a way to turn a talent into money, the concept of no free lunch is critical. It is rare that you will get someone to pay you something for nothing.

There is no free lunch.

The reverse is also true, and it is an error many people new to freelancing make. Your time and your talent are your products. Don't give them away for free. Part of becoming successful in this new paradigm is learning how to minimize the time you spend demonstrating your abilities in the sales process and how to shift to generating revenue. We will talk about this in much more detail in Part 3. Now, let's return to our morning mastermind session and meet some more people who have learned how to develop revenue from their talents.

I decided to attend this seminar on a bit of a whim—I had been following Peter Shankman on Twitter and happened to see his post promoting it. Since I didn't have a full schedule at the time, I thought it would be a good opportunity to find some new clients. It was at this session that I had the opportunity to meet Steve Woodruff.

I used to go to networking events in the hopes of gathering a big pile of business cards. The more cards I got, the more successful I felt. I worked the room, I kept my conversations short, I smiled and shook hands, swapped cards and moved on. Very little if anything came of all those conversations. Why? Because there was absolutely no relationship development. You can't get to know someone in 2 minutes—not in a meaningful way that allows you to understand them at a level that might help you build mutual interest. That is the real goal of networking. It is not about collecting cards, it is about finding the seeds of a relationship that might grow over time into something that has value for both parties. Therefore, I changed my goal and instead of shooting for the most cards, I started going to networking events with the goal of meeting just one person. I wanted to find, in a room full of strangers, just one person that I felt I could relate to. Someone I would want to meet again for coffee to find out more. Someone I hoped would become a core member of my network. In this case, that someone was a consultant named Steve Woodruff.

Steve's value proposition is unique. He helps people find their strength and turn it into a business. He is the master of developing revenue from talent. For Steve, the term "consultant" rings true for him in terms of how he works with his clients, but his mindset is that of a business owner. "Functionally I operate in a consultative way with my clients, but in terms of my view of life, I am always creating new things, and I think of myself as an entrepreneur." As an entrepreneurially minded consultant, Steve is also clear that he is not interested in expanding his practice and adding people. "I always intended to be just myself—I enjoy the freedom and the challenge that comes with being on my own."

For 10 years prior to becoming a consultant, Steve worked for a training and learning software company in the pharmaceuticals industry. His primary role was in sales and marketing—he was responsible for overall business development. However, like many smaller organizations, his company needed him to wear many hats. Rather than being limited to the sales space, he became involved with a variety of aspects of business operations including project management, and contributing to the design of the product itself. In sales you often have the most direct knowledge of what the customer wants, and even then, before he had truly considered branching out on his own, his mindset was already on how to increase the value of the product from the customer's perspective.

"It was a great opportunity to learn about myself and to identify things that I liked, things that I was good at, and things that our customers appreciated about my approach," says Steve. However, over time, despite the variety of working in a small company, Steve began to feel limited by his role. He started to think about how he could help people in a different way, to engage with them to solve a problem that his company was not specifically solving. "I always had a consultative approach and felt like that trusted role resonated with clients."

"I saw that my clients were having a great deal of difficulty finding and selecting vendors, and vendors were having difficulty finding clients. I realized that I was uniquely positioned to get in the middle and solve two problems."

There is a moment for most people who make a successful transition into consulting where they realize that they have something to offer that falls outside of the box of employment. Something unique and valuable that marries together a unique strength or ability, and a need in the marketplace. Steve had found himself in that moment.

You are probably thinking "lucky Steve" right now. After all, it seemed like he had his opportunity laid out on a silver platter—all he had to do was take it. However, the truth is that Steve was standing on a precipice. While he saw an opportunity to leverage his talents and break out on his own, he also recognized the inherent risk of simply grabbing that brass ring.

It is a moment of doubt for many freelancers because it means breaking away from the traditional "safe" path of being an employee. It means taking ownership for your own success or failure, and having the courage to take responsibility for your own results.

There are three big hurdles that he, like most freelancers, had to overcome in order to become an independent professional. The first hurdle is how to break away from your existing employer. For most of us, the talent that gives us the best opportunity to be successful as a free agent is the same or close to the same as the one we get hired for as an employee. Therefore, when you want to do work of some kind for a client that probably already has a relationship with your existing employer, it becomes a conflict of interest.

In all likelihood, you signed a contract or employee agreement that prevents you from doing work with clients of your employer, and it may even specify that your employer owns any work you produce while you are working for them, regardless of whether you do it as part of your job. This can be a sticky situation, and requires a great deal of finesse to navigate.

Steve had two choices—he could try to sneak around his boss and establish a relationship with some clients, or he could be honest and tell his employer he was ready to move on. The risks of doing work behind your boss's back are obvious. At best, you will likely lose your job, and at worst you could end up in a lawsuit, a solution that is in no one's best interest. However, being honest has risks as well. You could lose your job abruptly if your employer feels uncomfortable with the idea that you are considering this transition. If you have an employment contract that specifies that you are not allowed to solicit business from the company's client list, and your employer is not willing to bend on that, you may find that you are out of a job and have to take another job for a year or more until you can approach the clients you had in mind (by which time they may have found another solution for the need they were going to fill with your services).

Despite the risk of being fired, Steve had a conversation with his employer. He told his boss how he was feeling limited, that he was considering going out on his own, and that he was interested in pursuing a new challenge. Fortunately for Steve, he had an open-minded and supportive boss, who worked with him on a transition plan that gave him a substantial runway. While there is no guarantee that your company management will be as supportive, it is always better to be fired for being honest than to be caught being deceptive.

The possibility exists that the type of freelancing you plan to pursue is completely unrelated to your current job. If so, you are in luck, especially if you have no restrictions in an employment agreement that prevent you from doing work on the side. There is wide variation both by industry and by geography with respect to how moonlighting is treated. Software developers, for example, usually have strict language in their contracts that defines all inventions as the property of their employer. That means even if you are working at home, off hours, on your own equipment, you still may not own the results of your labor. Be sure you carefully read any agreement you sign, and check with your attorney if you are not sure what restrictions your employer may have placed on you.

The second major hurdle, after negotiating your exit from your current job, is cash flow. When you are developing revenue from talent, you will quickly find that your paychecks do not come as steadily as they did when you were an employee. This is not always a negative—often the checks are substantially bigger (although you will have to pay your own taxes and cover your own benefits, as we discuss in Chapter 8), but they won't necessarily come regularly, especially when you are just getting started.

"If I were going to do it again—if I could turn back the clock and redo my transition to consulting—I would make sure I had a paying client on the day I left my job," says Steve. He acknowledged that he had the permission and the opportunity to do so, but instead focused entirely on winding down at his work without building up his consulting portfolio. He launched his business on an idea, and the idea was a good one, but the sales cycle still takes time, and Steve admits that he put himself in a bit of a hole from a cash flow perspective during the transition. "It's not that it was terrible," he recalls, "but rather that it was unnecessarily stressful. I was worried in a way that I wouldn't have had to be if I had just gotten that first client."

And that leads to the third obstacle to the transition—the mental preparation. Many people I have met who are employees and would much rather be free agents are waiting for the right time. Early in their careers, people tend to worry that they do not have enough experience to be credible as consultants. Others feel like they need some magic combination of credentials in order to make the leap. Still others have mortgages, spouses, children, and financial pressures that make the risk feel too big to take.

Both Steve and I agree that there is no right time to make the transition. He had five children and a mortgage at the time he made the leap. Almost everyone has some financial worry, whether it is debt or cash flow or retirement. Certainly, the transition from employee to independent worker requires planning and a financial cushion if you can get one, but there will never be a perfect time to make the change.

4

Setting Up Your Business

In the last chapter, we talked about turning a talent into a revenue stream. However, knowing what you can do that has value to others is only the first step in making the transition from being an employee to working for yourself. No matter what skills you have that you are now going to turn into income, getting started as a freelancer requires a plan. In this chapter, we will cover the high-level steps of how to get started. In the remainder of this section, we will go into the details of how to accomplish these tasks. There are the steps to getting your independent business off the ground successfully:

1. Building up a financial cushion.
2. Setting up your business as a legal entity.
3. Establishing your brand and web presence.
4. Getting a client.
5. Doing the work.
6. Getting paid.

One of the main differences between working independently and being an employee is the fact that if you don't work, you don't get paid. So, prior to launching your business, you will want to have some money put aside—that much is obvious. The question is how much is enough? This depends quite a bit on your own financial situation, and your tolerance for eating ramen noodles.

Most people assume that you need to have thousands of dollars in the bank to be ready, but it is not necessarily about saving up a specific nest egg. What you need is cash flow to allow you to pay the bills and minimize the stress of the transition. There are two approaches to creating positive cash flow while you are making a substantial career change. One is to save money; the other is to reduce your expenses.

Understanding your own finances is a critical step in being able to work for yourself. Unfortunately, personal finance is still not something we teach in school, and some people who are looking to start their own businesses have no idea how to manage a personal budget. If this seems like it describes you, the first step you will need to take is to build a budget and shore up your knowledge of the basics of personal finance. You can do that by taking classes, reading books, or consulting a CPA, but I cannot stress enough the importance of understanding your own financial needs before you go out on your own as an independent professional.

Once you have gotten control of your financials and created a plan to stay solvent during the transition, you are ready to move on to getting your business set up, establishing a legal entity, and assembling a team of resources to help you stay on track. In the next chapters, we will talk in detail about each of these elements, but at a basic level, every freelancer needs to have three things in order to get up and running: a name, a business structure, and a bank account.

Having your business structure established and a bank account ready to take in your earnings, you can move on to setting up the other side of the business—your virtual storefront. While you don't need a physical space (usually) to do business as an independent professional, you do need to have a way to communicate with your clients, and these days that means a web presence, social media accounts, email, and a phone number. You will also want some business cards to remind the people you meet of how to get in touch with you.

While it is not essential that you have your marketing elements in place to land your first client, it will certainly help you to be successful over time. However, as we will cover later in this section, it is very likely that your first client will be someone you already know, possibly even someone you have done work for as an employee. This first client is essential to getting your business and your brand off the ground. Of course, once you land a client, you need to deliver your best work, send out an invoice, and make sure you take that first check to the bank.

These are the basics of the six-step process that every free agent goes through when getting started. It is the overview of the roadmap for success. However, in each individual case, the process plays out a little differently. In Chapter 1, we met Chris Brogan and learned how he went from a telecommunications specialist to the owner of his own consulting group. Now let's meet another successful independent professional who took a different path.

For Tammy Strobel, getting out of debt was the key to her transition from the corporate world to living and working the way she wanted to. Over the course of six years of downsizing and minimizing, Tammy went from living paycheck to paycheck as an employee to being financially secure as a freelancer.

In 2005, Tammy and her husband were two regular newlyweds with an apartment, two cars, and a pile of debt, living in California. Today, they live in a tiny house with just 128 square feet of space. For those of you in the corporate world, that is about the same size as 2 to 3 standard cubicles. In the course of their six-year transition, they downsized several times, progressively reducing their stuff, their living space, their debt, and their stress levels. In 2012, Tammy published a book called You Can Buy Happiness (and It's Cheap), in which she chronicled her transition from being an apartment-dwelling employee to being a free range, free agent writer and photographer.

The first seeds of what has grown into a full-fledged, flowering new worldview were planted in Davis, California about eight years ago. Tammy described it as being stuck in a cycle of unhappiness. "I was working at a job that wasn't a good fit for me, I was commuting two hours a day, I was in debt and I was shopping too much and things were just not good. I was really unhappy and just felt stuck in my life." Like many people, Tammy felt the uncomfortable combination of having so much and still feeling unhappy. "I knew that I was really fortunate and privileged to have what I had. Not everyone has a safe place to live and the ability to buy food and all of those things, but still I was frustrated."

As that frustration built, Tammy and her husband Logan began to have more and more conversations about living differently. They considered a variety of ways to break out of their rut—Logan was the first to suggest that maybe they should pare down their possessions. However, when faced with the idea of simplifying, Tammy was not so sure. "My husband Logan and I started talking about how we could change our lives for the better, and Logan suggested that we simplify. I didn't want to do that. I didn't want to give up my stuff."

Tammy wasn't alone in feeling that way about the things she had collected over the course of her life. The American Psychiatric Association estimates that over 2% to 5% of the population in the United States suffer from compulsive hoarding and that is only the few for whom it is truly a disorder. Of American households, 46.7% had credit card debt averaging $7,117 in 2013 and while that number is slowly declining, it is still a heavy

burden. Not only are most people accumulating more and more possessions, but also they are going into debt to do it. Tammy and Logan knew
they were going against the grain when they decided to live smaller, but
looking back now, she feels that the change has been a great one. "Seven
years later we're living in a tiny house and we're debt free. I'm a writer and
photographer, so now I'm just doing work that I really love and that reso-
nates with me and I just have a lot more time and space to not only engage
in work that I like but to spend it with the people that matter most."

Of course, it wasn't a simple transition. Tammy describes the process of
progressively scaling down over a period of years in her book. They shifted
to smaller and smaller apartments, working through a long slow phase of
eliminating things that were "wants" but not "needs." However, by taking
it slowly, Tammy says the habits become more ingrained and there was
less opportunity to backslide.

"We started simplifying in 2003 and we didn't get into our tiny house
until 2011, so we definitely took our time. I didn't de-clutter my life over-
night, it was a long process. I think that was better for us because our
behavior changed for good. I'm not sure if I'd downsized more quickly
whether I would have been able to keep those habits."

In addition to the process itself being a challenge, life continues to have
its own bumps and obstacles even when you are simplifying. In 2012,
Tammy spent much of the year being with her father as he battled a serious illness. She says that one of the biggest benefits of simplifying was the
flexibility it brought to her life. Without that, she doesn't think she would
have been able to take the time to be with her father through the final
months of his life.

"Five or ten years ago if my Dad had become so seriously ill, there's no
way I could have taken the time to help be his caregiver or to be with him
when he died and you know those are the things that I think people regret
when they look back. Why didn't I make that time? We've been intentional
about creating a life that's really flexible so there's that time for our family
members. And you know life isn't going to be perfect—it never will be but
you can build in a little resilience I think when you simplify." That resilience helped them weather multiple moves, the loss of Logan's job, and all
sorts of other challenges.

These days Tammy feels like their life has settled into a normal pattern. Normal, that is, for people who live simply in a tiny space. Tammy
spends her mornings focusing on writing, either for her blog or for her
next book. In the afternoons, she keeps up with social media and email,

but not having to commute makes it feel like there is much more time in each day. In addition, the flexibility to adjust to whatever comes up during the day works well, too. Tammy and Logan are currently living next door to her mother and helping her with various things. "Today during my lunch break we helped my mom take wheelbarrows of gravel into her garden. We're going through a process of renewing her garden and building that back up again, which feels really good. So taking four hours out of my day to do something like that isn't something I could have done 10 years ago, for example."

Moreover, it is a big contrast between Logan and Tammy's tiny house and her mother's 2,300-square-foot home. We talked about how comfortable the tiny house is in terms of heating and cooling, and because of the small size, it turns out the little space works better. "Tomorrow it's going to be 100 degrees. We have a mini-AC unit that keeps the house very cool, whereas my mom can't turn on the air conditioning to cool off her whole house because she can't afford it. It's an older house so it's so expensive. It would be over $400 per month during the summer and for us it's maybe $15. So for me it's a whole lot more comfortable here in the tiny house. We keep warm in the winter and cool in the summer."

Having traveled to other parts of the world, the Strobels have a strong sense of appreciation for what they have, even living as simply as they do. "These types of houses that we think of as so small, you know if you were in India you would see a whole family living in this amount of space. And it probably wouldn't be as nice. So I think it's really important to check our values. I think a lot of people have more than they realize here in the U.S. I spent some time in Mexico and I saw a lot of poverty and it just made me realize that I'm so spoiled you know, that my life is so good."

If you are thinking that living in a tiny house is sounding good right now, there are a few important things to understand about living super small. Most of the tiny houses from Tumbleweed and Portland Alternative Dwellings (PAD) are built on trailers in order to stay clear of building codes that apply to permanent homes. That means no connection to the sewer system, so you will gain an entirely new understanding of waste management. Most people who choose to live in a tiny house have composting or incinerating toilets, and there is a wide variety of models and systems from the simplest sawdust toilets to advanced incinerating systems costing thousands of dollars. The debate over the relative merits of each toilet system is always a hot topic on tiny house blogs, along with active discussions on every other aspect of small space living. It is a strong community and it allows anyone who is interested in the idea of living this way to benefit from a tremendous amount of research and information sharing.

We talked about the relative benefits of solar panels versus being connected to the electrical system. Tammy said they did some research and went with the grid because solar panels are a big investment. "We did a cost/benefit analysis with solar panels and they're so expensive. It's very inexpensive for us to plug into the grid. Our electric bill is between $5 and $25 per month. So with the air conditioning on this month it will probably be $15 or $20. We'll probably go the solar route eventually but right now we're holding off."

While Tammy and Logan hook up to the grid for electricity, and have running water in the kitchen, they don't have a shower. No shower? Well, they had an outdoor shower but quickly realized that in the winter that just wasn't feasible so they use the gym shower or borrow from family members. And while that may seem extreme, Tammy says there are ways to make up for anything. "My friend has a tiny house in Portland and she loves baths—it's one of the things she misses but maybe once per month she'll treat herself to a hotel that's kind of posh with a nice bath or a day at the spa and the nice thing is that you can do that because you have lower expenses. Sometimes I miss the shower but not all the time. And I certainly don't miss the rush hour traffic."

Despite the huge changes and the many things they have given up to pursue this lifestyle, Tammy has no regrets and really only sees the change as positive, especially in light of needing to be there to support her parents and her family through a difficult time. "Making the choices we have and then having our systems in place before shit hit the fan last year really helped. So I'm really grateful for that. And those beginning conversations when we were thinking about what do I want and what do I not need—they were really important for Logan and for me in particular."

Embracing change has become a lifestyle for Tammy and Logan, and they would recommend it to anyone who is just starting out down this path. "I learned so much last year and I continue to learn and move forward. But in terms of specific advice that I would offer to folks who are just starting out, it's just to be open to new perspectives and to have conversations with your partner and with your family about those short- and long-term goals and think about what you really want out of life. Because you know circumstances can change in an instant. I'm so glad now that I have the time to spend with my family and that I was able to take care of my Dad as he was dying and I think it's so important to really step back and ask yourself those big questions. It's overwhelming but if you can do that and then write down the things that are really important to you, you can start taking steps forward if that makes sense."

Now that she has made the changes in her own life, Tammy has come full circle and wants to help others find their way along this path. She considers herself incredibly lucky to be living the way she does, and being conscious about that motivates her to reach out with her story so that others can be inspired to change their lives if they want to. "I think it's about being aware of how fortunate you are too. I think if you're happy with yourself and your circumstances, you have the opportunity to help others as well."

While Tammy's extreme downsizing may not be for you, it is a good idea to reduce your expenses and minimize your debts prior to making the transition to working independently. The reality of income as a freelancer is that some months you may do very well and others may be dry. To level out those ups and downs, you will need to set money aside whenever you can. Starting with six months of living expenses as a cushion is a good rule of thumb, and it is easier to do that if those expenses are as low as possible.

5

Your Professional Team

When you are first starting out on your journey to independence, plenty of people will tell you that you need to have help. The few hundred dollars you spend (as hard as it is to scrape together when you are not making much, if any, yet) on the advice of professionals at the beginning of the process can save thousands upon thousands down the road.

For many, the biggest challenge of working for themselves is making enough money to sustain a reasonable standard of living. It can be hard to think beyond the threshold of subsistence, and the fact is that professional help and guidance does cost money. The good news is that it probably doesn't cost as much as you think.

With that said, what I hear from consultants and freelancers who are just getting started is that understanding the complex topics of corporate structure, let alone tax laws, liability, and insurance policy decisions, can be overwhelming. As I thought about writing this book and trying to provide some useful advice when I am neither an attorney nor a CPA, I seriously contemplated passing the buck and just writing a quick summary recommending that you go talk to these pros yourself.

However, as I spoke to people on both sides of the fence, current free agents as well as employed people thinking about going out on their own, I realized that this barrier, this fear of making a mistake had become a bogeyman of epic proportions. The idea that being an independent professional is somehow far more risky than being an employee is pervasive. We don't teach kids how to run their own businesses in school. Sure, lemonade stands are cute, but only for the very young. Once our kids grow up into middle and high school, everything they read and hear is about getting a job.

And later, after a few years of working, when the novelty of the cubicle and the water cooler have worn off, no framework exists to help individuals approach the alternative of being an employee—working for themselves. Therefore, my goal in this chapter is to sketch out the very basic elements of that framework, and to provide in a rudimentary form the key components of business management that you need to run your own business.

So let's get to know the roles of the lawyer, the accountant, and the insurance agent. They are the core of your professional team. They can provide you the things you need to stay out of trouble and allow you to focus on your work without the distraction of worrying about whether you are doing it right. Each one offers a perspective that is important for your success, but there is one critical skill that they all have to have if they are going to be part of your team—they have to be able to help you understand business issues in plain language.

In the simplest form, there are four big questions you have to be able to answer in order to be in business for yourself:

How am I paid?
How do I pay other people?
How do I pay my taxes?
What if something bad happens?

How am I paid seems simple—don't people just write you a check? They can, but if they write it in your name, you are at risk for being sued personally for the work that you do. So first, we will talk to an attorney about business structure, whether it makes sense for you to work under your name, or whether you should form a company, and if you form a company, what type it might be. Then once you have picked a business structure and gotten yourself set up with a bank account and a shiny business checkbook and debit card, your attorney will help you figure out how to work with your clients—whether you need contracts in place and if so, what those contracts say. If your business produces something like websites or writing, who owns the content when the job is done? Your attorney helps you stay out of the courtroom and helps make sure you are paid for the work you do.

How you pay other people and how you pay your taxes are questions for an accountant. Doing it right means that you can avoid a visit from the IRS (which no one wants). Understanding how to manage your business so that you minimize your taxes as much as possible is the best way to get back every penny you spent hiring that accountant. Working as a team, your accountant and your attorney help you make good decisions and avoid pitfalls and disputes with your customers.

Finally, helping you figure out how to protect yourself from the ups and downs of the business world is your insurance agent. What is the most valuable thing you own? If you thought of your house, your retirement savings, or even your car, you missed something much more valuable— your ability to earn money. Let's say that you make an average of $50,000 a year over the course of a 40-year career. That is $2 million dollars—quite an asset! Your insurance agent's job is to help you figure out how to protect your income and your business from whatever might happen, but also to help you decide what type of insurance makes sense. Because we are all different and the work we do is more or less risky, it is not possible to say what type of insurance you might need. But on the plus side, most insurance agents will help you figure all of this out at no cost to you (other than the price of the insurance premiums themselves).

Let's begin with the first question that every freelancer needs to answer before taking on their first piece of work: how are you structuring your business?

CORPORATE STRUCTURE

In September 2012, two partners running a brewing company in Denver, Colorado called Strange Brewing had the experience every business owner dreads—they got a cease and desist letter from an attorney. The problem? The name of their company was similar to a shop called Strange Brew Beer & Wine Making Supplies located nearly 2,000 miles east in Marlborough, Massachusetts. The letter accused them of infringing on federal trademark rights and insisted that they stop using the name immediately.

For better or for worse, the Internet era has made the world a little smaller, and while you or I might not think that there is any problem with two beer-making enterprises located far away from one another sharing similar monikers, the law disagrees. After multiple rounds of negotiation between the parties, as well as Facebook campaigns by supporters, and fear and anxiety on the part of the founders, a compromise was found but it is a cautionary tale that reminds us to do our homework when choosing a business name.

As I sat down with several attorneys to learn more about what freelancers need to know to run their businesses, I heard a variety of similar stories. From a back of the napkin offer of equity ownership that took a six-figure lawsuit to resolve, to disagreements over ownership of content written for websites, legal issues for small and solo business owners run the gamut. It is one of the things that make people nervous about going out on their own. However, fortunately there was plenty of good news in these same conversations.

Business law is complicated, certainly, but with just a few basic structures in place, independent professionals can minimize their risk and sleep well at night. The issues fall into three basic categories—corporate structure (what kind of business you run), contracts (how you set boundaries and guidelines with your clients), and copyright/trademarks (who owns what). In this chapter, we will go through each of these in detail so you know what questions you need to ask, and can make smart decisions about how to set up your business.

As we talked about in Chapter 2, one of the complicated parts about the trends in self-employment is related to the fact that some independent workers are incorporated while some are working under their own names as sole proprietors. Because there are so many different ways to work outside of the realm of a one-to-one employer/employee relationship, the decisions can be complicated.

The most basic decision that has to be made is whether to work as an individual or whether to incorporate and operate as a business. To help understand the difference between the two, let's talk about a particular independent professional and see how it works for her.

Caroline is an instructional designer. She creates e-learning courses using a piece of software called Storyline. She has a home office and buys her own software tools, her own computer, and uses her mobile phone to communicate with her clients. Caroline gets some of her business from referrals, but most of the work she gets comes from a relationship with a company that uses her as a sub-contractor (let's call them LearningCo). A big Fortune 500 company hires LearningCo to produce its learning products for a flat fee. LearningCo in turn calls up Caroline and negotiates with her to do the work for an hourly rate. Caroline sends LearningCo an invoice and it pays her by check in her name. At the end of the year, she receives a 1099 from LearningCo for the total amount it paid her over the year.

This makes Caroline a sole proprietor. She reports her earnings as business income on Schedule C of her federal tax return (as well as the correct form for her state taxes). She can deduct the cost of her home office, computer, software, and phone as business expenses, and the resulting income is taxed as self-employment income.

It seems simple enough, so what are the risks and downsides of being an unincorporated sole proprietor? The main issue, and the reason most independent professionals choose to incorporate, is personal liability. Let's say that Caroline is in a rush on a project, and she copies a course that is copyrighted by someone else. She changes the logos and sends the course off to her client as a finished product. The original owner discovers this violation and sues the client, who in turn sues Caroline for copyright infringement. Because Caroline is a sole proprietor, the lawsuit can go after her personal assets including her house and any other money she has to settle the suit.

Incorporating creates a separation between you, the person, and you, the professional. A corporation creates a boundary between the things that belong to the company and the things that belong to you individually. Therefore, for Caroline, if she were incorporated, the lawsuit could only include the money in the company bank account, as well as anything else in the name of the company.

That sounds like a better plan, right? It does and it is, but there are a few things to know before you head off to file your paperwork.

First, if you choose to incorporate, you have to run the business like a business. If you just file your corporate documents, but run all your business earnings through your personal checking account, the court will treat you as if you were a sole proprietor. The official legal term is "piercing the veil," which is a complicated way of saying that you mixed up your personal finances with your business finances. If the courts cannot clearly tell which is which, they may decide that you cannot claim the protection you thought you were getting by incorporating. So, if you do choose to go that route, make sure you get what you came for by setting up a business bank account, keeping a set of books for the business, and then paying yourself as if you were an employee. Is it more complicated? Yes, but if you are doing any kind of work that opens you up to liability, it is definitely worth it.

The next hurdle in deciding how to run your business if you decide to incorporate is which type of structure to choose. There are three main types from which to choose, and each one has benefits and drawbacks depending on what you are trying to do. I will explain them all here, but this is where you can really get a lot of value out of talking to an attorney who understands your exact situation. However, before we get into the matter of structure, there is one step you have to take first—you have to pick a business name.

Corporations are created and regulated in a couple of different ways. Each state has its own office that oversees businesses operating out of or registered in that state. For most, it is a part of the office of the Secretary of State. In the Appendix, you will find a complete list of the websites for corporate registrations by state, but it is easy enough to do a quick web search to find out where to register your business. No matter what type of structure you are going to choose, the first thing you will need is a unique name. Almost every state has a database you can search to make sure your name is not the same as one that already exists.

Why is this important? Let's say I spend several years and quite a bit of time and money establishing myself and my brand under the name KatyCo. Then one day, I find out that someone else has a company called "KatyCo" in the town next door, and people are confusing them with me. To avoid the inevitable issues and lawsuits that would ensue, states require each business to have a unique name. Using the state database will help you make sure the name you want to use does not overlap with anyone else's in your state. However, what about the rest of the country? What if I thought I should call my company Microsoft or Walmart? While there might not be a company registered in my state under that name, it would still conflict with a major corporation.

The U.S. Patent and Trademark Office maintains a database called TESS (Trademark Electronic Search System), which will allow you to search the national database by name and make sure you are not overlapping with someone else's brand. Another way to find out who else is using that name is to look on the Internet. I went to www.katyco.com and discovered that a company based in Barcelona is using that name related to a line of children's clothing. Good thing I didn't really name my company that! Finding a unique web address can be a challenge, but it is also a great way to find a unique name that is not in use by anyone else. Odds are if you can register a domain name with the business handle you want to use, it is probably not going to conflict with anyone else, but you should still check with the federal and state databases to be sure.

Once the matter of a unique name is settled, you will be on your way to deciding what type of structure you want to use. There are three primary choices:

C Corporation
S Corporation
LLC

Whenever I see these three together, I am reminded of that old Sesame Street song—one of these things is not like the others...

The C Corporation (or C-Corp for short) is different from an S-Corp or LLC in one obvious way—how it is taxed. C-Corps are the only corporate structure where the company itself pays taxes. What does this mean? Let's go back to Caroline and imagine for a minute that she decided to incorporate as a C-Corp. All she would need to do is file the paperwork (getting some help from her attorney) and pay a filing fee. She would be issued a Tax Identification Number (TIN), and then she could have LearningCo pay CarolineCorp instead of writing the check directly to her. When tax time rolled around, CarolineCorp would pay taxes on those earnings (minus any expenses), and then Caroline could take all the profits as a dividend. She would have to pay taxes on those dividends, too, which results in the problem of double taxation.

If CarolineCorp earned $100,000 after expenses, and paid around 30% in corporate taxes, she would have $70,000 left over. If she took that as a dividend and paid 25% in taxes on that (these are estimates, so check with your accountant for exact amounts), she would pay an additional $17,500, which leaves her with only $52,500 of her original earnings. C-Corps are corporations that pay their own taxes based on their income or losses first, and then the owners pay taxes on money if they take it out through dividends.

For those of us who operate alone, a C-Corp may be more than we need from a corporate structure perspective. Unless you plan to have investors and raise money, most independent professionals gravitate toward either the LLC or the S-Corp because of the pass through taxation.

What is pass through taxation? It is simply that the tax burden of the company passes down to the owners directly as income. If Caroline decided a C-Corp was not for her, she could choose an S-Corp. In this case, the $100,000 that CarolineCorp made would, after all of the business expenses were deducted, be reported as income to the owner or owners. If Caroline was the only owner, she would be responsible for paying taxes on 100% of the income. She would have to pay self-employment taxes as well as income tax, but there would be no corporate tax paid first. An LLC works the same way—the only tax paid is at the personal level by the owners. We will talk much more about taxes in a moment, but for understanding how business structure works, the first difference to understand is how they are taxed.

Why else might Caroline want to incorporate? Another reason is purely for marketing purposes. If Caroline goes to pitch a client in hopes that it will hire her, it will want to be sure that she has the capacity and the skills to do the work. If she goes in under her own name and offers to do the job, her potential client may rightfully be skeptical about whether she alone can do a big job; it might worry with a longer-term project that she might get a job and not be available. However, if she goes in as Caroline, president of A1 Instructional Design Corporation, she may appear to be more stable because she is presenting herself as a business rather than as a sole proprietor.

Because everyone's situation is different, there is no way that a book can tell you what is right for you and your business. However, what you do need to know is what questions to ask and what things to think about when you are working for yourself. Here are some of the most important questions to talk about with your lawyer.

1. What Business Are You In?

Depending on what you do, you will be more or less at risk for being sued, and will have more or less need for contracts, business structures, etc. So, helping your attorney understand exactly what services you provide, for whom, in what context, and for what compensation is the first step in getting good advice. Preparing for this conversation means sitting down and documenting some of those elements. It is a good idea to be able to describe your typical client (even if you don't have one yet), your typical engagement, and what product you will be producing or selling.

2. Who Do You Work With?

For most independent professionals, it is a one-on-one relationship between you and your clients. You propose to do a piece of work, you negotiate a fee, you do the work, and you send your client a bill. However, sometimes you may do work with other people as part of a larger project, or your work may be sold to others after you sell it to your client. Describing this workflow and process, even if it seems trivial, is helpful to your attorney as he or she works with you on defining your business operations. It is especially important if you have partners or others who are going to be part of the corporate structure. There are limitations, for example, about who can be listed as an owner of an LLC vs. S corporations.

3. How Will Your Business Income Impact Your Taxes?

Taxes are a topic for both your attorney and your accountant. One of the most important things to understand about your business structure, as we talked about earlier and will talk about more in the next section, is how it affects your taxes. If you choose LLC or S corporation, and your taxes pass through to you, you will have to know how much money you make after you have paid all of your expenses. However, if you choose a C corporation, the business itself will be responsible for its own taxes, and then any income you make from the business will be taxed separately.

4. How Does the Business Structure Itself Protect You from Liability?

No one (that I know of) goes into business with the intention of being sued. Yet, 43% of small business owners report either being threatened with or involved with a civil suit. Therefore, while you have every intention of running your business in an honest and aboveboard way, being protected from liability is one of the main reasons to think about forming a corporation. In addition, beyond the corporate structure itself, your contracts and anything you sign that governs the work you do for you client should be structured to limit your liability as much as possible. An attorney who understands what you do and how you do it can help you create a template and review things before you sign them to make sure you are doing everything you can to reduce your risk. It is not possible to entirely eliminate liability, no matter what. If you are driving a car on company business and you hit a pedestrian, both you and your company will likely be on the hook. It is a complicated topic, and for many people, this is where it gets so confusing that they throw up their hands in despair and skip the whole process. If you have been tempted to do that or even if you have been running your business without legal advice up until now, now is the time to talk to someone. While there are complexities, that is why the attorneys make the hourly fees they charge. They understand it all and can explain it to you in plain terms, as it applies to your specific situation, and give you peace of mind.

6

Finances and Accounting

Once you have established a relationship with an attorney and figured out the best structure for your independent business, the next member of your team should be an accountant. Accounting at its most basic is the process of keeping track of the money you earn and the money you spend as you go through the process of operating your business. There are two key elements of running a successful business as a free agent from an accounting perspective. First, keep business and personal expenses separate, and second, keep track of every dollar you spend or earn.

Keeping business and personal expenses separate may seem like a no-brainer, but when you are first getting started, it is actually tough. If you are the only employee of your business, it may seem ridiculous to open a bank account in the name of the business, deposit checks there, and then take that money right back out again to put into your personal account and pay the bills. This is where you will benefit from getting help from an accountant.

Record keeping is the key to everything you do when you are self-employed. As we will see in a moment when we move into talking about taxes—the most critical financial issue a freelancer faces—keeping accurate and comprehensive records of every dollar you spend will help you reduce your taxes and stay out of trouble with the IRS. There are several ways to go about record keeping, from the very simple (keep all of your receipts in a shoebox) to the high tech (apps on your smartphone to record and track your receipts, manage your mileage, and take payments for your work). However, before any of the high-tech options can add value to your business process, you need to know what you are trying to track.

Selecting an accountant is similar to selecting an attorney; in fact, your attorney should be your first stop if you are looking for someone to work with you on your business finances and don't know anyone personally. Ask for recommendations from your lawyer as well as any other freelancers you know. Once you have a short list of candidates, check their credentials. Business accountants should all hold a CPA (Certified Public Accountant) credential, which demonstrates that they have taken course work and passed an exam. While this does not guarantee that they are either competent or reasonable people, it is certainly a good place to start. Most CPAs will be willing (outside of certain times of the year when they are exceptionally busy with tax work, specifically March and April) to have a free initial consultation. This is a great time to go beyond the credential and find out whether they are used to supporting independent professionals, and whether they seem like they understand your business.

Many CPAs are also self-employed, so for most, the work they do for you is the same work they do for themselves. Working with an independent accountant has the benefit of growing your network as well as getting solid advice about managing your own business, so do not feel like you are better served working with a larger tax firm. Often, the smaller groups or independent individuals will have more reasonable rates, and will be able to refer you to other professionals as you need them to grow your business.

When thinking about accounting practices for your freelance business, there are several key processes to keep in mind:

1. Maintain a separate bank account.
2. Track mileage and expenses.
3. Invoice clients in a timely manner.
4. Stay on top of accounts receivable.
5. Pay your taxes.

BANK ACCOUNTS

In the last section, we talked about setting up your business as a legal entity, which gives you the ability to set up a bank account in the name of your business. Why would you want to have a separate bank account if you are the only one working? There are several reasons. First, having a bank account for the business makes it easier to keep track of business income and expenses. When you do work, you bill your clients, and when their payments come in, if you deposit them into your business account you can easily run reports on your total income.

If you run all of your business expenses through your bank account, it makes your life much easier when tax time comes around. As we will see in the next section, business income is reported on your personal federal taxes on Schedule C. In order to calculate your net income, you have to be able to show all of the money that came in, and all of the business expenses that went out. If you are running all of your business expenses through your personal bank account, it can be a big job to separate business expenses from personal expenses.

In addition to complicating your taxes, putting your business income into your personal bank account weakens the protection of your corporate structure. If you incorporate your business as an LLC, but cannot show a clear separation between your business and your personal finances, you may risk having your personal assets come into play in the event of a lawsuit. The legal term for this is "piercing the veil" and it is not something you want to do.

Another reason to keep a separate bank account is for credibility with clients. When clients write a check to you in the name of your business, they feel like they are working with an established and stable operation. It is a good way to demonstrate that you are a serious professional, rather than someone who is just moonlighting or working independently for the short term.

Finally, having a separate bank account is a way of establishing a credit history for your company. If you need to apply for a loan or have a company credit card, you will need to be able to establish that you have a consistent flow of income, and that you pay your bills on time. While you can secure loans with your personal credit, it is better for the separation of your business and personal finances to have the business itself be seen as credit-worthy.

TRACKING MILEAGE AND EXPENSES

If you spend time driving to visit clients, or even if you just go to the bank for business purposes, that is an expense that you can deduct from your income, which lowers your taxes. If you have made the choice to open a business bank account, half the job of tracking expenses is done. However, the other half—tracking expenses that do not come directly out of your bank account—will still need to be accomplished. Tracking your mileage can be time consuming. It involves keeping careful records of every mile you drive for business, as well as the total mileage you drive each year. Either you can track your mileage by keeping a simple log in your car or you can use tools that are more sophisticated.

There are a variety of mileage tracking apps for iPhone and Android, and many of them will use the GPS data from your phone. So, all you need to do is hit "start" when you head out, and "stop" when you are home again. The IRS sets a standard mileage rate each year (in 2014, it was 56 cents per mile). At the end of the year, you multiply all the miles you have driven by that rate and you will have a nice big deduction to lower your taxes, but only if you keep track of all those miles throughout the year.

INVOICING CLIENTS IN A TIMELY MANNER

Depending on how you price your work, you may invoice by the hour or by the job. However, either way, if you want to be paid on time, you need to get your invoices out on time. This is easy if you only have one or two clients, but it can get unwieldy quickly as your business grows. As we talked about earlier, your invoices should have your business name on them, as well as payment terms. The standard payment term is net 30, which means your client has 30 days from the date of the invoice to pay you. If you do not send out the invoice on time, you risk having a problem with cash flow.

To help you keep on top of your invoices, you will likely need to use bookkeeping software. These tools can be tremendously valuable in terms of helping you keep track of payments you receive, allowing you to report on your expenses, and helping you see where the money is going. There are many such tools to choose from, including Intuit's Quicken, Freshbooks, Mint, and others. Your accountant may also recommend a particular tool that he or she prefers.

STAY ON TOP OF ACCOUNTS RECEIVABLE

Once you have sent out your invoices, you have to wait for a little time to pass before you can call on your clients and ask them where your payment is. While some clients may pay quickly and without a problem, it is inevitable that you will have a client that does not pay on time, or does not pay at all, without a reminder. This is another area where having a software tool to help you stay on top of your business processes can be a big help.

An aging report is a report that allows you to see what invoices are out, what their due dates are, and which are overdue. You need to be in the habit of checking the aging of your invoices regularly, and if you see that you have not been paid, follow up promptly. Cash flow can be a big challenge for freelancers, especially when the business is just getting off the ground. So making sure you are on top of your accounts receivable, and making sure that you are being paid correctly and on time is important for your success.

Accounting is all about keeping track of your income and outgo as you run your business. One of the most important reasons for good accounting practices is because taxes need to be paid correctly and promptly. Taxes are a complex topic, so in the next chapter we will delve into how to calculate your taxes and how to pay them correctly.

7

Paying Taxes

Author's Note: This chapter is about taxes, so it may be both the most important chapter in terms of staying out of trouble and the most mind-numbingly boring chapter in terms of content. Either way, the information here is meant to help you understand some of the differences between paying taxes as an employee, and paying taxes when you work for yourself. I am not a CPA (although I did have several tax specialists review all of this information to make sure it is accurate) and everyone's situation is different. The goal though, is to provide you with some context for how taxes work when you are self-employed, and some terminology so you know what questions to ask an accountant.

Because many people have little or no financial training as part of their formal education, I have written this chapter at a beginner level. If you have quite a bit of experience managing your finances, you can skip ahead, I won't mind. However, if you do not know much about taxes, we will start at the beginning.

As a rule, dollar for dollar you will pay more taxes as a freelancer than you will as an employee. We will see why when we get into a few specific examples, but the basic reason is that, as a free agent, you will pay both the employer and the employee portion of the taxes collectively known as FICA, which includes contributions to Social Security and Medicare, among other things. So, overall, you will likely pay a higher percentage of tax on your income, but tipping the scales in the other direction, you can also deduct quite a few things as business expenses that you can't deduct as an employee from the income that you earn. The cost of driving to a client, for example, is deductible as a mileage expense, as are tolls and parking costs. Quite a lot of the costs associated with running your business, including paying your accountant, your lawyer, and any other professionals who help you run your business, are also business expenses that directly reduce the amount of income on which you will be taxed.

To see how these factors work in practice, let's get to know a couple of fictional people who will help demonstrate the differences between employees and free agents in the world of finances and taxes.

Jack is a marketing specialist at BigSoftware, a high-tech company based in Big City, U.S.A. He has worked there for 5 years, and earns $60,000 per year. He has a full set of benefits including health insurance that is 80% paid for by his company, a 401k plan with a 3% match, and he gets 15 days of paid time off every year.

Jill is a marketing consultant who works out of her house just outside of Big City. She has been freelancing for about 5 years. Jill has five clients, each of whom pay her $1,000 a month, which means that her income is coincidentally also $60,000 per year. Jill pays for her own health insurance, and has an IRA account for her retirement savings.

Over the course of this chapter, we will talk about how Jack and Jill handle their finances, and you will see where there are similarities and where there are some big differences in how they operate.

Before we break down Jack and Jill's monthly pay, let's define a few important terms:

Payroll: This is how employers pay their employees. Payroll is usually paid weekly, biweekly, or monthly, and many deductions come off the top before you get to the amount that ends up in your bank account. A paycheck includes several elements including:

> **Gross Pay:** The total amount of your salary divided by the number of times you are paid per year. So, Jack makes $60,000 per year, and if his company pays him monthly, his gross pay is $5,000 per month.
>
> **Deductions:** From that $5,000, quite a few things are removed or deducted from Jack's total salary. Some deductions are mandatory, including federal income tax, state income tax (if it applies in your state), and FICA (which we will talk more about in a moment). Others are optional and might include things like Jack's 20% contribution to his health insurance plan, as well as his contribution to his 401k.
>
> **Federal Income Tax:** When Jack started his job, he filled out a W-4 form on his first day, which told his employer how much tax he wanted them to take out of his check every week. Because Jack is single and lives in an apartment, he listed

zero exemptions on his W-4. He should have used a tax calculator to figure out how much to have deducted instead of going by the form because (as we will see in a minute) Jack is going to owe money to the IRS at the end of the year.

State Income Tax: Depending on what state you live in, you may or may not have to pay income tax.

FICA (Federal Insurance Contributions Act): This deduction refers to the amount of money taken out of your check to contribute to government insurance programs including Social Security and Medicare. As an employee, you pay half of the FICA tax and your employer pays the other half. As a self-employed person, you are both the employer and employee so you pay both halves.

In 2014, Social Security tax was 12.4% of wages up to $117,000 (this amount changes annually), and Medicare tax was 2.9% with no income limit. Because Jack is an employee, he pays 50% of that and his employer pays the other 50%. Jack sees a deduction for Social Security and Medicare on his monthly paycheck that adds up to 7.65% of his total income.

Exemptions:	1
Income:	$60,000
Adjusted gross income:	$60,000
Standard or itemized deduction:	$10,000
Taxable income:	$50,000
Total tax credits:	$0
Total tax:	$8,429

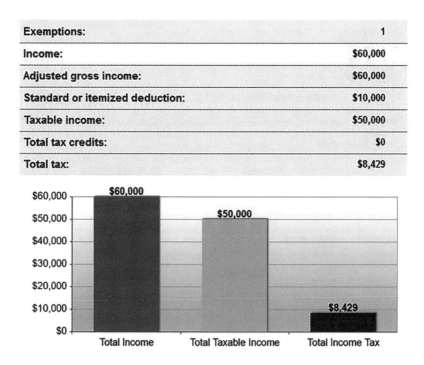

As a freelancer, Jill pays both halves, or 12.4% for Social Security and 2.9% for Medicare, but just to make it confusing, only on 92.35% of her income. Therefore, the total FICA tax for self-employed individuals like Jill is 15.3% of their income up to $117,000, and 2.9% after that. The big difference is that Jill gets all $5,000 paid to her by her client each month, and she has to write a check to the IRS to pay her taxes. Jack's taxes come right out of his paycheck and he never sees that money in his bank account.

Jill, on the other hand, gets the full $5,000 paid directly to her. Her clients withhold nothing. She has a contract to work for $100 per hour and assuming for our nice coincidental calculations that she works 10 hours per month for each of her clients, she will invoice each of them for $1,000 and they will pay her that amount. It is now her job to figure out how much of that to set aside to pay taxes (we will talk about how to pay those taxes in a minute).

However, fortunately for Jill, she will not pay taxes on all of that income because as we mentioned before, she will deduct business expenses from what her clients pay her, and that number (known as net income) is the

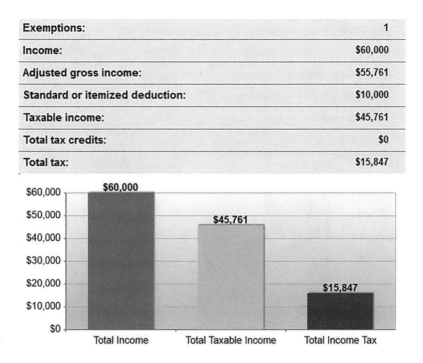

Exemptions:	1
Income:	$60,000
Adjusted gross income:	$55,761
Standard or itemized deduction:	$10,000
Taxable income:	$45,761
Total tax credits:	$0
Total tax:	$15,847

one she uses for her taxable income. Business expenses can include a variety of things. Here are a few of the most common:

Mileage
Parking
Tolls
Accounting fees
Attorney fees
Computer hardware and software for business
License fees for business
Home office deduction
Office supplies

If Jill uses her car to drive to her clients' offices to do work, her mileage is deductible using the IRS mileage rate of $.56 per mile. If she buys a computer or needs software to support her clients, she can deduct that, too (all of which she has double-checked with her tax accountant to be sure they are truly deductible). Her tax will be figured based on her net income—her income after expenses.

Exemptions:	**1**
Income:	**$37,000**
Adjusted gross income:	**$34,386**
Standard or itemized deduction:	**$10,000**
Taxable income:	**$24,386**
Total tax credits:	**$0**
Total tax:	**$8,440**

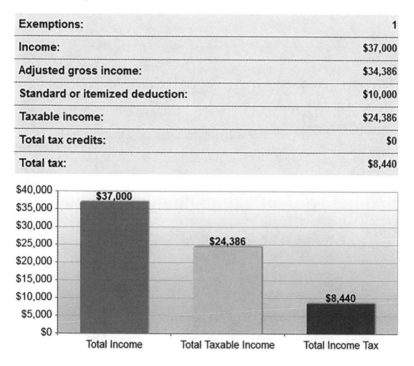

Jack is definitely bringing home more money each month if we simply compare their income equally. So why would Jill choose to freelance instead of choosing to be an employee?

Let's go back to Jill's client base. We said she was making $1,000 from each of her clients, but we did not talk about how many hours she is working. If her billable rate is $50 per hour, she needs to work 20 hours for each client in order to make $1,000. That is 100 hours per month. Jack, on the other hand, is working approximately 172 hours per month, plus a commute. If Jill were to work the same number of hours as Jack, her income would be substantially higher.

The purpose of this comparison is not to give you precise numbers so much as it is to show some differences between how taxes work for employees as opposed to free agents. Here are a few of the main differences:

1. Overall taxes are higher for self-employed people because they have to pay both halves of the FICA cost.
2. Self-employed people can deduct some expenses like the cost to drive to and from client sites where employees cannot.

Exemptions:	1
Income:	$72,000
Adjusted gross income:	$66,913
Standard or itemized deduction:	$10,000
Taxable income:	$56,913
Total tax credits:	$0
Total tax:	$20,330

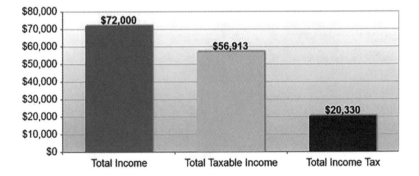

3. Using a SEP IRA, you can put away more money for retirement (which is deductible from your federal taxes).
4. Having to pay for your own health insurance is a substantial cost, but is also deductible.

In addition to having to know how much to pay, you also need to know how to pay it because if you wait until April 15 of the following year without paying what are called estimated taxes by the IRS, it will hit you with a substantial penalty for underpayment.

The IRS provides an electronic system called EFTPS, which allows you to schedule direct electronic payments and pay your estimated taxes out of your bank account on a quarterly basis. Payments are due four times per year on the following dates:

April 15 (for the period January 1–March 31)
June 15 (for the period April 1–May 31)
September 15 (for the period June 1–August 31)
January 15 (for the period September 1–December 31)

You will notice these are not exactly in quarters—the June payment only covers two months while the January payment covers four. The goal is to estimate your net income over that time period, and then use the tax calculator provided by the IRS to decide how much to put aside.

As a rule of thumb, independent professionals should put aside approximately 30% of every dollar they earn toward taxes. In most cases, this will be more than you need, but if you are just starting out and need a guideline, it is a good place to begin. If you know how your income will fluctuate throughout the year, and you want to get ahead by paying more into the system earlier in the year, that is one way to be sure that you have covered your tax burden.

I cannot stress enough how important it is to keep track of what you earn and what you spend. I mentioned it at the beginning of this chapter, but it really cannot be said often enough. When it comes to reducing your net income and paying out as few of your hard-earned dollars as possible, nothing is more important than knowing what you earned and what you spent.

Finally (although perhaps most obviously), the small amount of money (relatively speaking) that you spend on a competent CPA to advise you at tax time and to answer your questions throughout the year is one of the best investments you can make.

I honestly do not know anyone who looks forward to paying their taxes, but I do know that having the tools and the knowledge you need to accomplish this critical task will keep you from having sleepless nights filled with nightmares about IRS auditors.

We have talked about setting up your business correctly, about paying your taxes, and about keeping track of your expenses. In the next chapter, we'll cover another key part of setting up your business—protecting your income from the unexpected.

8

Insurance and Risk Management

Insurance—The dictionary will tell you that it is "a practice or arrangement by which a company or government agency provides a guarantee of compensation for specified loss, damage, illness, or death in return for payment of a premium."

Unlike the business structure conversation, it is not that people don't know what insurance is, it is more that people don't always know what they need, where to get it, or how much to get. As a rule, insurance is something you pay a small amount for that protects you against an unlikely and expensive event. The biggest challenge for free agents is finding an insurance agent or company that will cover you as an individual. Why is that? Well, mostly, it is about probability.

Not to give you flashbacks to your 5th grade math class, but the underlying principles that underpin how insurance works, how it is priced, and what it covers are rooted in probability. It is easy to find statistics on how often something happens. In any given year, for example, you have a 1 in 700,000 chance of being struck by lightning and, over your lifetime, those odds are 1 in 3,000. In theory, then, if you put 3,000 people in a room, you could say that one of them would be struck by lightning in their lifetime.

How do we know that? Well, every year the number of people reported struck by lightning gets entered into a database somewhere, and over time we see that while that number might go up or down in any given year, as a percentage of the population, it stays fairly constant. In fact, almost every type of event happens, over the entire population of the country or the world, at some known rate that we can see from history. Insurance companies track these statistics because it gives them half of the information they need to set rates for insurance policies. Where does the other half come from? It comes from the cost that results from the event taking place.

Let's use an insurance industry example. The National Fire Protection Agency keeps track of how often houses burn down. Between 2007 and 2011, approximately 1 in 320 houses experienced a fire. Each year, an average of 366,600 homes experience fire, causing an average of $7.2 billion dollars in damage. That tells us that the average house fire causes just under $20,000 in damage. The U.S. Census Bureau tells us that in 2010 there were 114,800,000 households in the country. Therefore, a quick trip to the calculator tells us that if every household paid $63 a year to an insurance company, that would cover the cost of all of those fires. That is how insurance companies set their rates (of course, they tack on a little for administrative overhead, profitability, and such, too.). The cost of all the damage to all the possible homes, spread out across all the people who might possibly experience that event results in a premium rate that ensures that the person with the insurance will have the money he or she needs, whether it is $10,000 or $100,000 or $1,000,000, should his or her house burn down. All the insurance company has to do is hold the money and verify that the insured person actually did have a fire.

So with that in mind, let's think about insurance related to being employed. There are two main types of risks related to working independently, and we will talk about those first before we go on to talk about health insurance. First, there is the risk of becoming unable to work, and second there is the risk of being sued for something related to the work you have done.

RISK 1: BECOMING UNABLE TO WORK

As an independent professional, your ability to earn income relies almost 100% on your ability to do work. If you can't work, you can't get paid. If you get hurt or sick or otherwise lose your ability to do the work you do, you will have to rely on disability benefits from Social Security, which will likely be much less than your working income. While no one wants to think about becoming disabled, according to the Social Security Administration, just over 1 in 4 of today's 20-year-olds will become disabled before age 67. That is quite a bit more risky than being struck by lightning or having your house burn down, so it makes sense to invest in insurance to mitigate that risk.

There are two types of disability insurance—short-term disability and long-term disability—which work in concert to provide you income during times in your life when you might be unable to work. Short-term disability usually covers less than a two-year period of disability, and often much less (60 to 90 days). Long-term disability then kicks in and covers you over the course of many years if your disability lasts that long. Policies often differentiate between disability due to accident and disability due to illness. What does this mean? It means that you should read your policy carefully and make sure you choose to get the coverage you want and need. Nothing is worse than thinking you will be covered in a certain situation, having that situation happen, and then finding out you are not covered.

There are many questions to ask once you find an agent willing to sell you a disability policy, but often the hardest part of the process is finding someone willing to sell it to you. That is because covering individuals takes away from the simplicity of the math we talked about earlier. Let's go back to our fire example. If a carrier could cover every single household in the United States, it is likely that it would see results that were fairly close to the statistical probability of fire and damage estimates. However, for most insurers, they are only covering a small portion of those houses. In addition, in some cases, that small portion happens to be in an area where fires happen more often, or where the home values are higher, and because of that, they have to adjust their rates to account for the difference.

The same is true about covering individuals in the insurance marketplace, which is why many insurers will not do it. Insurers have the best chance of coming out ahead if they can predict the likelihood of a particular event happening in that population. If you are an army of one, they have no idea how likely it is that you personally will become disabled, or how much income you will earn over any given period. The reason disability rates are low for large companies is because the insurance company can look at it as one large population and try to predict what its risk of having to pay out will be. For independent workers, this just is not the case.

Your first challenge, then, is to try to find an insurer who will work with you, and one of the best ways to do that is to make yourself part of a group. Often industry associations, chambers of commerce, and other groups of independent professionals or small businesses join together to form a larger pool. In these cases, insurers are willing to write policies because the group is large enough to suit their statistical needs. However, even when you find an insurer who is willing to write the policy, there are some things to watch out for:

1. Occupation. Let's say that you are a graphic designer. If you became blind, you would certainly not be able to do your design work anymore. However, you might still be able to do other work, and as such, your insurance company might tell you that your benefits will stop and you will have to get another job. This nuance is referred to as "own occupation." If your policy covers you for your own occupation, it must cover you if you cannot do the job you were doing at the time of your disability. If it covers you for "any occupation," that might sound better, but it is actually worse. It means that it only covers you if you cannot do anything. Keep your eye out for policies that change after a period from own occupation to any occupation. This is something you will want to avoid if possible.

2. Waiting period. This is a little like the deductible on your car insurance. The shorter the waiting period, the more the policy will cost you. If you can build up a solid emergency fund and keep a cushion, you can afford to have a longer waiting period, which can save you money on your premiums.

3. Percentage of salary replacement. You will see a number regularly when you look into disability insurance, and that is 60%. Many policies have a standard benefit of 60% of your gross income. At first that might seem like too little, but if you are paying your own premiums, your disability insurance payments will not be taxable. In addition, you will likely not have commuting, clothing, or other job-related costs while you are disabled (although you will probably have higher healthcare and other bills, so this may not matter). Deciding how much of your income you want to replace is a balance between the cost of the insurance and the benefit it will pay.

4. Term of coverage. Short-term disability policies range from a few months to a few years, but rarely longer than that. Long-term disability policies will either specify a term (10 years, 20 years, etc.) or will specify an age where they will stop providing benefits (55, 60, 65, etc.). An ideal policy provides benefits until your retirement age so that you can smoothly transition from disability insurance to a combination of Social Security and retirement funds.

5. Renewability. As with many life insurance policies, most disability insurance policies are (or should be) guaranteed renewable as long as the premiums are paid. You do not want to have to renegotiate the insurance every year or run the risk of having the policy canceled before its term if you have paid into it faithfully.

One of the keys to getting a disability policy is a stable income. If you have just started consulting and your income is highly variable, you may not find an insurer willing to write a policy that covers you at the peak of your income level. In a best-case scenario, you will have an insurance broker by your side to help you navigate the process. However, even with a knowledgeable expert on your team, you still need to understand as much as you can about the process to make an informed decision. So, do your homework and learn the terminology.

You also may (frustratingly) find that you get different answers from different people. You may talk to several brokers and hear different answers about what is available and how much it costs. You may hear that something is possible from one source and then find out that it is not. In addition, people may tell you things verbally, but without having it in writing you may not get that price or feature in your final policy.

So check and double check, be persistent, and know what matters to you!

The risk of being unable to work is closely followed by the risk of being involved in a lawsuit related to the work you do. This risk is broadly referred to as liability, and as a person working independently, you will need to decide to what degree you have liability in the work you do, and then find out if it is worth the cost to mitigate that risk.

RISK 2: LAWSUITS

Interestingly, quite a lot of attorneys are self-employed, and while none of us ever thinks we are going to be involved in a lawsuit, the sheer number of cases and law practitioners implies otherwise. And just as with the risk of your house burning down, or you becoming disabled, the risk of being involved in a lawsuit is a statistic that is tracked by the insurance industry. In fact, insurance companies devote a huge amount of time and money to analyzing the relative risk of lawsuits across various types of work, and set rates accordingly.

Liability insurance comes in two main forms:

1. Errors and Omissions—This type of policy covers you for mistakes you might make in the course of your work that might cost your client money. For example, let's say that you are an accountant. In the heat of tax season, you make a mistake that results in a huge fine from the IRS

to your client. That client, rightfully upset because he or she hired you for your expertise, sues you. Think of it like malpractice insurance for freelancers and you won't be far off the mark.

2. General Liability—This is also occasionally called slip, trip, and fall insurance. General liability policies cover you for accidents and injuries that happen in the course of your work or at your place of business. This can include things like someone falling down the stairs when they come to your office for a meeting. It can also include injuries related to the work that you do. Let's say you are a photographer and as you take your client out to a spot you selected for a photo shoot, he or she is stung by a bee and has an allergic reaction. While it might seem ridiculous for you to be the target of a lawsuit, it has certainly happened.

One of the most common liability concerns for creative freelancers is the matter of copyright. If you are in the business of producing either creative writing or visual design, the question of who owns your work at the end of the project can be a thorny one. Copyright law says that the author owns the product by default, but there are a number of exceptions and ways you can, deliberately or accidentally, give away your rights. If you work under a contract where you are producing "work for hire," the product that you create will legally belong to your client. If you used that work for another client, you can be sued.

Lawsuits are expensive, time consuming, and can cause irreparable damage to your reputation as a professional. While a good contract should do the heavy lifting of protecting your rights, the risk of a lawsuit is always present in the business world.

Insurance is a layer of risk management, but it is not and should not be the only layer. When we talked about contracts, we talked about indemnification—the idea that your client releases you from liability for your work. While you will not always be able to remove all liability through your agreements, you should be able to limit it. Furthermore, having the right corporate structure protects you from personal liability. If you are working as a sole proprietor, a client can sue you and your personal assets such as your house or your retirement savings can be fair game. However, if you have a corporate structure, the lawsuit should only be able to include the assets of the business.

9

Pricing, Proposals, and Contracts

Like a law of nature, whenever two or more independent professionals come together for lunch or coffee, the subject of setting rates will naturally come up. Putting a price on your time and your work is more than just a matter of throwing together a proposal; it is a question of value. As an employee, there are salary benchmarks for your value that are well known and widely accepted. It is a bit like checking out the Kelley Blue Book to find out what your car is worth. If you know your job title, how many years of experience you have, and where you live and work, you can find plenty of data on what you should be paid. Being a free agent is somewhat different and the range in rates, rate structures, and payment processes varies tremendously.

I recently asked two different graphic designers to bid on designing a slide deck that I planned to use as a business development tool. I needed some basic artistic design, a nice color scheme, some stock photos, and a few font choices. I sent both designers a draft of the deck, along with the requirements that I just listed.

The difference between the two quotes was over $15,000, which is quite a range! How is it possible that two freelancers, given the same general project description, could come up with such drastically different estimates? The answer helps us understand the art and science of creating proposals and setting rates. First, let's look at the basics of how the designers approached the process.

Designer 1 came in with a quote of $21,590. She based it on an hourly rate of $190, and an estimate of 3 hours per slide, along with a budget of $200 to $500 for stock photography.

Designer 2 came in with a quote of $5,000. She based it on an hourly rate of $75, and an estimate of 1 to 2 hour per slide and a budget of $250 for stock photography.

Freelance and contractor hourly rates do vary widely. The first clear difference between these two estimates is simply the hourly rate. At $190, Designer 1 is definitely on the high end of the rate scale. How can she possibly expect to win any business if there are other designers willing to work for $75 per hour?

- Client Budget—If you are working with big companies, they often have big budgets to match. It is not always true, but in most cases, the bigger the client, the higher the rate. Tiny companies and startups tend to be incredibly cost conscious. With little money to spend, they want to get the most out of every dollar. Larger organizations expect to pay higher rates, but also expect consultants to have great references, be available on their schedule, and have plenty of expertise.
- Opportunity for Work—For a small piece of work, if I know it is unlikely that a potential client will need more, I usually charge on the higher end. But if there is a good chance for long-term work, and especially if it is work that I am particularly interested in doing, I might charge a lower rate.
- Client Load—If I have a full schedule, I will often bump up my rates when I am sending out new proposals. That helps in two ways. First, if I get the business while my schedule is still full, I know it will be worth putting in the extra time. Second, if the client takes a while to sign and my workload is lighter, it will help keep my income stable.
- Convenience—If a client is located 5 minutes away or if the majority of the work can be done remotely, I will also consider a lower rate because I can fit the work in between other clients and be more efficient with my time.

Across all types of independent workers, rates range from less than $10 per hour to more than $200. So, setting the right price for your services is very much an art. For many first-time freelancers, it starts with the hourly rate they were making as an employee. A graphic designer making $75,000 per year who decides to go out on his or her own can do a quick calculation and see that he or she makes about $37.50 per hour. Why not charge that? It is easy to justify—you can tell your client that you cost the same as an employee it could hire.

There are just a few problems with that plan:

1. Benefits—As a freelancer, you will have to pay for your own health insurance, disability insurance, and fund your own retirement. You have all of the risk and no safety net from unemployment.
2. Overhead—Working on your own means you are not only the person doing the work, but also the sales and marketing department, the accounting department, and the office administrator. You will need to spend money to make money so things like business cards and software and other tools will come out of your pocket. The good news is you can deduct it from your taxes, but it does take away from your take-home pay.
3. Dry Spells—Whether you want to work a full schedule or not, sometimes you won't have paying clients. Every independent professional goes through times when they don't have enough work to do. When that happens, you will need to have a cushion in your bank account, and that cushion comes from charging a higher hourly rate.

If you want to use the hourly rate calculation, most freelancers I know take that $37.50 per hour and double it, charging $75 per hour, and that is most likely what Designer 2 did.

While this calculation makes great logical sense, it is not truly based in the value of the work. While it does assess the value of the hours the designer is putting in, what about the value proposition to the business? Let's say that I am going to go out and pitch a $1 million dollar deal with this slide deck. I am going to want it to be powerful, to deliver my message in a way that my potential client can't fail to see that I am the right choice for it. I am going to want original art, strong clear graphics, and a great flow.

If that is the case, it is well worth the $190 per hour and the extra time per slide. I am going to want to know that I am working with someone exceptionally talented, creative, and willing to go above and beyond for this project. There will probably be extra communication and revisions, as well as various rounds of feedback on artwork and colors. At that level of intensity, and ideally for a presentation that wins a huge piece of business, I would be more than willing to pay the $21,000.

This is a typical value proposition in business consulting, and if your specialization is helping companies grow, manage through change, or become more profitable, it is likely your rates will be at or above the $200 per hour mark. Why? Because success and value are measured in terms of the value to the business. If working with a consultant for three months improves the bottom line by $500,000, it is worth quite a bit to the business owner to achieve those results.

But how and when do you make the value case? Is it best to withhold rates until a second or third conversation, or to be up front and risk losing the work before you have a chance to make your value proposition clear? How much free consulting should you do in the sales process to prove your skills before you start charging for your time? Should you provide some sample work for free or hold out for the signature on the contract?

The consultants who have been working for themselves for a long time are adamant—set your rates higher than you think you should for both of the reasons above. First, because you need to make enough money to do more than scrape by or you might as well go back to being an employee. Second, your work has real, tangible value to your client. If you price yourself too high, you risk losing clients who can't afford your services, but if you set your rates too low, you risk not having the time and positive energy you need to do the work at the level it should be done. While I never mentioned the capabilities of the two designers in the previous example, you probably assumed, as your potential customer would, that the lower priced designer was likely to provide lower quality work or exhibit a lack experience.

PROPOSALS

Since we are talking about pricing, this is a great time to talk about how you put your value proposition in front of your potential client. Your proposal is a structured document that you use to describe what you are going to do, and how much it is going to cost. A great proposal does the job of convincing your client that you are the best person for the job. To do that, it needs to include several important components.

About Your Company

This section is where you reinforce all of the reasons that this particular client can and should choose to work with you. The moment of decision about which vendor to hire usually comes after everyone has made their pitches in person, and then has left behind their marketing collateral along with a pricing sheet or proposal with the costs of the work. No matter how impressive you were in your presentation, what you leave behind will likely be the only thing in the room representing your expertise when the prospective client gets down to comparing proposals. Therefore, you had better be sure that you clearly, professionally, and expertly highlight your capabilities in a way that keeps your value proposition at the top of your prospect's mind.

Scope of Work

In this section, you lay out exactly what work you are going to do. If you are responding to a formal Request for Proposal (RFP), you may have a cookbook set of tasks to draw from, but if not, this section forms the basis for your project plan. The scope of work is one of the most critical components in your proposal because this will be the basis for the prevention of scope creep.

What is scope creep, you ask? Experienced freelancers will tell you that scope creep is the biggest potential risk to an otherwise lovely relationship with a client. It is the difference between what you thought you were being engaged to do, and what the client thought it was going to get from you.

In 2008, a small nonprofit organization decided that it wanted to overhaul its website. They had historically used the web as a simple contact form and to give prospective donors, clients, and volunteers a little information about their mission, service area, and founders. With a $2,500 grant from a local community donor, the executive director engaged a web designer to work with them on updating the site.

As they sat down to discuss the needs and goals of the new website, the designer and the executive director created a detailed list of features that the site should have. Among those features, the word "calendar" appeared. After an hour or so of discussion, they agreed that all the features the organization needed could be built within the budget specified.

A few weeks later, when the designer presented the first draft of the design, she proudly demonstrated the calendar function. Click on this button and a calendar appears—you can include events and let people know right on your website what is going on in the organization. Sounds like a calendar, right?

"How do people register to volunteer?" asked the executive director, brow furrowed. The designer paused.

"Register?"

"Yes, the calendar needs to allow the volunteers to sign up for events, and the system needs to confirm and ideally send them reminders when the date is coming up. It needs to show us how many people have volunteered and how many slots are left, and we should be able to send out automatic emails to let people know which events still have spaces open. Doesn't the calendar do that?"

This is scope creep. When the executive director said "calendar," she actually meant that she wanted a fairly robust event management system, but because she was not a technical person, she didn't realize that her idea of a calendar, from the perspective of someone who manages a large group of volunteers, was quite different from the designer's idea of a calendar—a simple place to display events by date.

If we could roll back the clock to the day of their original meeting, what would we suggest that the designer do to better understand the scope? What should she have said that would have prevented this communication gap?

"What do you mean by 'calendar'?" would have been a great question. The clearer you can be when you write up your scope of work (and when you price a project), the less likely you will be to run into a significant scope gap. However, since our friend the web designer and her client can't roll back the clock, what can they do?

Having a conversation about a change of scope can be difficult, especially if the client is now faced with the unpalatable choice of either paying more or getting less than she expected. And while the easiest choice—simply offering to do the work for free—may be what your client wants to hear, it is not usually in your best interests as an independent professional to do a significant amount of extra work without getting paid.

If at the original meeting, the designer and the executive director had discussed this functionality in detail, the consultant could have shown the difference in cost between a simple calendar and various levels of functionality in terms of allowing registrations to events. However, having that conversation after the contract is signed and expectations are set is a big challenge. Therefore, the best bet is to be as detailed as possible in drawing up the scope.

Pricing and Terms

The last section of the proposal after the scope of work is the pricing and terms section. You have a choice when you create a proposal—some freelancers include all of the terms directly in the proposal including payment schedules, nondisclosure, and other clauses that would typically be part of the contract (which we will talk about in just a moment). This type of proposal can simply be signed by the client and then becomes the contract.

While this has its advantages in terms of efficiency, the legal language can take away from the focus on how your services are directly solving a problem for your client. The goal of the proposal is to do everything in your power to convince your client that you understand and can exceed its needs and goals for a reasonable price. If you make this case well, and it accepts your proposal, the client will already have the motivation it needs to work with you on negotiating the contract. If, on the other hand, you present your potential client with several pages of terms and conditions, it may be put off (even if it knows these clauses are important and will ultimately be a part of the negotiation).

As a rule of thumb, proposals should come first and should focus on the specifics of the work and the cost. If your client accepts your proposal, then it is time to move on to a contract.

CONTRACTS

One of the most common questions that comes up around freelancing is whether you need to have a contract in place with your clients. I have heard hundreds of arguments for and against the concept of a contract, and because there is no requirement to have one, and because getting a contract drafted often requires the use of some of those precious dollars of income to get a legal review, many freelancers go without.

Some of the most common reasons for not having a contract are:

"A handshake is good enough; I trust my clients."
"I'm just giving advice, what do I need a contract for?"
"It's too much of a hassle for the client to go through a contract negotiation, and I might lose the deal because of it."
"I don't know what to put in a contract."

No matter what excuse they use, the real reason most independent professionals avoid contracts is because they are generally written in legal language, and it is expensive to get lawyers involved with what might be only a small piece of business.

In the best of all possible worlds, you will only do business with reputable clients who pay on time after the first invoice you send, and who will agree with the way you want to deliver your services. Since most of us don't live in that best of all possible worlds, contracts are a really good idea for many reasons. First, let's go through the terminology because demystifying the language goes a long way toward making the process less painful.

Contracts, Agreement, and MSAs (Oh My!)

For most independent professionals, these three things amount to the same thing. Contract and agreement are both words for a legal document that outlines terms that both you and your clients agree to in a formal sense, meaning if you or your clients then break those terms, the other person can take them to court. A master services agreement (MSA) is slightly different in that it defines terms and then allows you and your client to have separate work orders that refer back to the overarching MSA. If you plan to do multiple projects with a client, this would be a good choice because then you don't have to go through the process of renegotiating the contract each time, you just write up a work order or statement of work (SOW) that refers to the terms you already agreed to in the master agreement.

Nondisclosure or Confidentiality Agreements

Many clients will want you to sign a nondisclosure agreement (NDA) or confidential disclosure agreement (CDA) in order for you to even have a conversation with them about their needs. Typically, these short documents only cover the fact that your potential clients are going to tell you something or show you something that they don't want shared with anyone else. As we will see, your contract should include nondisclosure as well, but often if clients want to tell you about their business, they will ask you to sign a separate NDA first and then will expect a contract next.

These are the main types of agreements that you will see as a freelancer. Typically, if you are working with a large company, it will have a contractor agreement that it will expect you to sign (and you should definitely have your lawyer review it). With smaller companies, they will generally ask you to send them your standard agreement and then they will have their attorney review it.

While many people will tell you that the whole reason you should have an agreement in place has to do with avoiding being sued, that is not actually true. A well-written agreement is a foundation document that sets down in writing your expectations of your clients, as well as what they can expect of you. I try to make my agreements as friendly as possible from a language perspective both for myself (so that if the clients want to make changes, I understand completely what they are changing) and for my clients so that they know how the relationship will work. A well-written contract should start by covering the following points:

Who—The very first line of most contracts includes the names and legal addresses of the people involved. That should be you (listed by your LLC if you have one) and your client (listed by its legal name and address). This clearly defines exactly who is involved in the process, and whom you should go to if you have any problems.

When—Most (all?) contracts have what is called a term. That is how long the contract is in force. Just like the President, your work has a term limit that starts on a specific date and runs for a set period. Moreover, with a term comes a termination process. This is usually a full section of your contract that says who can end it and under what circumstances. In many cases, either you or your client can end the contract with some notice (30 days is common) but other contracts may say that you can only end it if one or both of you breaks the agreement in some way. This part of the agreement is one that you will want to understand in detail. In addition to the term, your agreement or the work order that goes with it should define, roughly, when the work will be carried out. Will you be meeting with the client every day? Once a week? Will you be providing updates? How often? Setting clear expectations about when the work will be done will keep you from having difficult conversations later. No client wants to hear that you have other client work to do, so setting a schedule that allows you to meet their expectations while juggling your other priorities has to be done at the beginning of the project.

What—Whether it is specifically included in the contract or attached as a work order, your agreement should spell out what type of work you are performing, what the deliverables are, and how you and your client will decide when the work is complete. One of the most important things you can do to set yourself up for success is to write a clear, specific, measurable scope of work so that both you and your client know what is included and what is not. This is an art in and of itself, and I will cover it later under project estimating.

Where—If you think you are doing most of your work from home, and your clients think you will be in their office each day, you will be off on the wrong foot before you start. Conversely, if you need space to work in their office or access to specific tools, files, people, or data, it is good to make sure that is covered in your agreement.

How—Every engagement is different. A web designer will have an entirely different process for producing his or her end product than a management consultant. However, since your clients may or may not understand how your process works, it is up to you to help them know what to expect when working with you. Can they call you every day as often as they want? Do you charge extra if you work off hours? Do you charge for travel, parking, or tolls? Any detail that you want to be sure is understood belongs in your contract. Here are a few examples of details you will often see:

1. Payment Terms—Your contract should tell your clients when you are going to invoice them (ahead of doing work or at specific milestones or when the work is complete) as well as how long they have to pay the bill.
2. Expenses—What expenses will be billed back to your clients? Do you charge them for equipment or for other supplies? If so, is there an approval process?
3. Status Updates—While some clients are not picky about status updates, others will want formal reports on a regular basis. Make sure you know what your client wants and that you are comfortable providing it.
4. Project Manager—Will your client be assigning a specific person as your point of contact or will you be working with a team? This is an important point and one that has the potential to take a lovely engagement to a dark and unfortunate place. If multiple different people at your client can re-prioritize your deliverables, you risk being stuck in the middle of ugly office politics. Having a defined project manager can help you avoid that pitfall.

The goal of a contract is to define the terms of the relationship. While the list we have just been through is quite comprehensive, a good contract does not need to be hundreds of pages long. An efficient attorney can cover the basics within just a few pages. The important part is that both you and your client thoroughly understand to what you have both agreed.

10

Getting Your First Client

When you look at independent professionals as a group, more than half are over the age of 35 and the largest cohort (more than 45%) are over the age of 45. For many, it is because they built up a lifetime of skills and contacts, and then parleyed that into income. However, the fastest growing segment of the self-employed population these days is in the 20- to 34-year age range. This group, which represents the millennial generation, has shown a strong interest in entrepreneurship and independent work, not as a career capstone but as an intentional lifelong earning practice.

A 2011 survey by Young Entrepreneur Council and Buzz Marketing Group found that 27% of millennials are self-employed. Because of the poor economic conditions that were in place when they graduated from college in 2007–2009, some opted out of the job market and started up their own businesses. Moreover, even those who took jobs are continuing to pursue their own work on the side. Thirty-five percent of employed millennials are also running their own businesses when they are not at work.

This path can be harder than getting started mid or late career because many 20- to 30-year-olds have not yet built up a network or portfolio to help them have credibility and get clients.

Alexa Johnson is a photographer. She is smart, personable, and most importantly (at least for the sake of her independent career goals) stubborn. At 16, she started taking photos as a hobby and it grew into a passion. In high school, she packed her senior schedule with art classes to build her portfolio, even winning awards for her pictures. When she applied to college, her dedication and talent were obvious to the admissions teams. She was accepted at every institution she applied to except one.

"I was excited," Alexa says, "I had never been told that my talent and my art were valuable and important. I really felt like I was on my way to a great future."

Alexa enrolled at Montserrat College of Art, but after one year, she left, disenchanted with the way that school had made her passion into a chore. "It was too structured," she told me, "It took all the joy out of the work for me."

Coming home after a year in school, Alexa was determined to become a professional photographer. She did research, built a website, found a mentor, and started taking free work to build her reputation. But it wasn't easy. Her friends and family continually questioned her for not taking a job. However, in her work, and with her mentors, she had found the creative outlet she wanted; she just needed a break to make her dream a reality.

Living and working in a vacation community, she knew her best market opportunity was in wedding and event photography. But how do you get your first job? It is a question that challenges even seasoned freelancers, but for someone with few connections and a portfolio still in its infancy, it was a serious problem.

Alexa needed wedding pictures. She needed to prove that she could take exceptional photos so she could attract clients in a competitive market. But without a client, she was stuck.

Until she got creative.

She and a friend bought a cheap wedding dress off the rack. They used the fabric but created a new, modern design using sewing skills they both had from high school. She recruited some friends and ordered inexpensive dresses for the "bridesmaids." When the dresses didn't arrive, they had to fall back to pencil skirts and white blouses. They prepared for months as if for a real wedding, assembling flower arrangements and driving around to spot great locations for their photo shoot.

Their hard work paid off—not only did Alexa get great shots to use as marketing materials, she got the experience of dealing with real-world scenarios. Learning to deal with stress, developing contingency plans when people or dresses didn't work out, and still turning out a great result were part of a growth experience that Alexa now says was key to her success.

While people questioned why she would spend time, energy, and money on this project, she knew it was a risk she had to take. Nothing ventured, nothing gained.

Getting a first client isn't the only hurdle a newly minted independent professional faces. At first, Alexa didn't know much about contracts or negotiations with clients. Some clients tried to intimidate her, counting on her relative youth to think they could push her into working for free or reducing her rates. Others pushed back on how she used their photos for her own website, and even a logo designer tried to stake a claim on her branding.

The learning curve was steep, and particularly so because as a young professional, Alexa didn't have as many professional contacts such as attorneys or insurance specialists who might have pointed her in the right direction to avoid some of these pitfalls. However, even without all the support and guidance she might have wished for, Alexa still had her own determination to push her through the hard times.

These days Alexa feels like she is well on her way to establishing herself in the marketplace. She has worked incredibly hard to get her business up and running and she knows there will be more hurdles to overcome, but she is still as fiercely committed to this path as she was in the beginning.

"I can always go get a job," she says, "that option will always exist. But if I don't fight and persevere and pursue what I truly want, there's no way it will happen. Could I go to work in an office and get a steady paycheck? Sure, but I would always feel like I was missing out on doing the work I want to do."

She still works to expand her skills and her repertoire. The variety is what interests her—the idea that every day presents a new challenge, every job has its own new learning opportunities.

"It's more about confidence than anything else," she says in closing, "When you are doing something on your own you have to have your own confidence. Everyone else will tell you what you should do and they are not always supportive of you following your path. But in the end it's your life and you have to make those decisions yourself even if it isn't what someone else would do."

It helps to be surrounded by people who are supportive, too. In learning the trade, Alexa met other photographers and creative professionals in the course of her work. Seeing others who shared her passion helped her feel less like her path was strange. Still, it is surprising that so many people question the legitimacy of working independently when more than 25% of the U.S. labor market is self-employed.

Last year Alexa organized and participated in a charity event. She and a group of photographers, make-up artists, and hairdressers got together and invited girls to come into the Harwich Community Center for a photo shoot. The participants dressed up, had their hair and makeup done, and then received a professional photograph. It wasn't a huge event, but it was another way for Alexa to creatively market herself while doing the work she loves.

Getting your first client is different for every freelancer. For some, that first client is a friend or colleague—someone who has seen your work and knows its value. For others, it will be a total stranger who found you through word of mouth or through your marketing materials. No matter how you get your first client, you will need to learn from the process so you can continue to build your portfolio of successful business relationships.

We talked a lot in Part 1 of this book about the factors that make free-lancing an attractive career path—the flexibility to work where and when you want, the ability to do the work you really love, and the potential to make a great living. However, in order to make the transition into work-ing for yourself, there is a hurdle you have to overcome—you have to find someone who is willing to hire you.

The first client is the most critical—it is what establishes you as a consult-ing professional and what starts to build your referral platform. It is also often the thing that helps you believe that you truly can be successful as an independent professional. Your first client is the proof point that shows you can make money off your talent, independent from an employer.

Landing that first client can be a big challenge though, and being successful in getting someone to pay you for your skills that first time requires a little ingenuity. Most likely, your first client will be someone you know well—it may even be your current employer. In this chapter, we will explore strategies for landing that all-important first gig.

Back in Chapter 3, we met Steve Woodruff, a consultant who not only makes money through creating links between vendors and their custom-ers, but who also helps independent professionals define and refine their own value propositions. You may recall that Steve's one regret in how he transitioned from employee to consultant was that he didn't have a client in place when he went out on his own.

This is a key factor, and a critical tipping point for your success. It has to do with an important fact in marketing yourself: the sales cycle.

The sales cycle is the length of time it takes from the moment you first meet a prospective client to the time you receive your first payment from them. Sales cycles can be as short as a single day. If you are in the right place at the right time, and you strike up a conversation with someone who has purchasing power, you may be lucky enough to get a signature and even a deposit during the very first encounter.

This is extremely rare.

For the most part, your sales cycle will be measured in weeks or even months. While everyone's business is a little different, the process is universal.

First comes the awareness phase—this is how you make people aware that you exist and that you offer a service they might value. In a shorter sales cycle, this will often amount to people you know or customers you have done work for before. They already know that you are there, and they already understand what you do. If they are coming back for more, it is usually because they found value in your services. While your best customer, especially in the early stages of your new venture, is likely someone you already know, you can't count on this being the case.

Building awareness of your services, your value proposition, your brand, and your pricing is a process that is usually referred to in general terms as marketing. Marketing is all about getting a message out to an audience to tell them about your services. Many people assume that marketing and advertising are the same, but while advertising is an extension of marketing, something you may or may not do depending on who and where your customers are, marketing is something everyone does, and extends from how you define your services to the look of your proposals, all the way to what social media platform you use. We will talk in much more depth about the tactics of branding and marketing in Chapter 14, but for now it is enough to know that in order to get a client, the person who will write you checks and support your lifestyle, you will need to work on building up awareness of your service offerings. You do that by marketing yourself.

Marketing activities can include everything from attending networking meetings to advertising in industry publications to speaking at events and conferences. Your goal is to make the people who would benefit from working with you aware that you exist, and that you are available and willing to work with them. If you have done that successfully, you will move on to the next phase of the sales cycle, which is usually a meeting or a phone call to define the opportunity.

Defining the opportunity means transitioning from a general conversation about what you do to a more specific discussion of what your potential client needs, and how you can help. One of my first clients was a small services firm based in Avon, Massachusetts. Avon is the home of one of the most successful home furnishings chains in New England—Jordan's Furniture. Launched by a pair of entrepreneurs, Jordan's created a new paradigm for furniture sales, building an experience-based destination store. Its huge facilities were themed, included restaurants and rides, and in later iterations, IMAX movie theaters.

Jordan's Furniture is a prime example of marketing and branding. It observed a need in the marketplace, a frustration with the status quo, and built an entire service operation around the customer experience.

My client was just a few blocks away from the iconic Jordan's building, and the difference between the two organizations could not have been more dramatic. The small, dim offices paneled in dark wood contained cramped desks with no visual or auditory separations. Every conversation could be heard not only by every member of the office, but also by the customer on the other end of the phone. The atmosphere was strained, the equipment dated, and the overall impression was that of a company stuck in the command and control management philosophies of the 1950s.

I had been invited to meet with the owner and his wife to help them figure out how to scale the operations of the business. To my extreme surprise, when the owner of the business came into the conference room, he was full of life and sparkle. He talked about his passion for customer service—his fundamental belief that their competitive advantage lay in the quality of their technicians, their commitment to servicing their clients at the highest level, and their thorough understanding of modern techniques. In other words, their physical working environment was the polar opposite of their corporate ideals.

We talked through the challenges their organizations faced. I listened to the passion and the goals that the owner had for his organization. This is a sales call, and your goal is to find out as much as you can about what the needs are for this person and this organization at this moment in time. Their goal is to find out about you, your experience, what you bring to the table, how you work, and whether you are the right person for the job.

For many independent professionals, this moment is incredibly stressful. It is easy to feel like you are on trial, sitting in the spotlight having to prove that you are capable of doing the job and that you deserve to be paid anything at all. However, being anxious is not going to get you the job. In fact, the most successful approach involves a different mindset altogether.

When I entered that cramped, dark office, I had one goal in my mind: to help this company find the resources it needed to be successful. I certainly recognize that my skills and capabilities are on that list of resources, and that I may be the one who can help them. But my goal, and I say it straight out in the beginning of the meeting, is to figure out the right solution, even if it is not me, to help them.

This is a credibility building process. I am here because this organization has a challenge and it needs help. I am here because I have said something to someone earlier on in the process that got me the meeting. I am here to gather the information I need to truly understand the problem, and to be able to propose a solution using my skills and talents or to refer them to someone else who can help them in a way that I can't.

It is a simple shift of mindset, but it is critical to winning not only your first client, but also every other engagement you have. The closer an opportunity is to your unique skills and value proposition, the more valuable your help will be.

Why am I talking about this in a chapter about getting your first client? Does this seem like something you won't need to know until you have many clients under your belt? In fact, this is the biggest mistake that many people who are new to the independent working paradigm make.

They take the wrong work.

If you go into an opportunity, and especially in the early days of your first few clients, you may feel this way, desperate to close a deal no matter what that deal may be, you will be taking the wrong work, and you will be shooting yourself in the foot instead of getting off on the right one. You should be as picky about your clients as your clients are about working with you. Your best opportunity of success lies in finding a client that not only you can help, but also help beyond their expectations. The perfect first client is one that will be so thrilled with your work that they will go out and tell everyone they know about you, and about how you helped. A great first client is one that asks for a stack of your business cards at the end of the engagement so they can tell their friends about you.

That will never happen if you are so desperate for a client that you talk them into working with you even though it is not the right fit.

So, here you are in your first client meeting. You have asked all the right questions, you have heard what they want and what they need, and you believe sincerely that you are the absolute right person to help them tackle their business problem. The next step is the proposal.

I mentioned earlier when we were talking about marketing that the proposal is part of the marketing process. That is because your proposal should be designed to do two things. First, it should describe in detail the services you are offering to your client, and second it should demonstrate why you are the right person for the job. You would think that after meetings and conversations, you would not have to continue to sell yourself at the proposal stage, but the truth is that the moment that the deal is most likely to fall through is the moment of decision and commitment. Up until that point, it has been all talk and the risk of lost time has mainly been yours. However, when the clients sign, they are committing at least money and possibly time as well. So it is at that moment of decision that your message needs to be front and center to remind the prospects of all the reasons they need your help.

However, in order to get the opportunity to send a proposal, you have to have the ability to attract clients in the first place—a big hurdle for many independent professionals who are just getting started in the business.

11

Networking and the Art of Getting More Clients

It's noon on a Wednesday and spring is not yet fully in bloom on Newbury Street in Boston's Back Bay. In another month, the patios will be filled with tables and umbrellas, and the crowds will be out in force to shop and eat, and to see and be seen. But it is still only April and a brisk wind is blowing off the water, so we're holding our monthly meet-up indoors.

There are six of us around the table, each an independent professional, representing a variety of services and fields of interest. Michael, who used to work for a huge publishing company, is describing how he got here.

"I worked for a big company for a long time," says Michael, and then after a pause, "way too long."

He was comfortable at the big company—the paychecks came without fail every two weeks, he had a space to call his own, a cubicle in an open space, coffee in the kitchen, steady (if uninspiring) work. But after 17 years, he made the first transition from a company of 30,000 to a company of 30.

There is a very different dynamic in a small company. You know everyone. There is no nameless, faceless bureaucracy to deal with; it is all people that you work with every day. You can see each part of the business, and you can see change happen. Small companies are a completely different ecosystem—where most people have one very narrow specialization in a large organization, they tend to wear many hats in a smaller environment. It was a rewarding and refreshing change.

Two years later, Michael paired up with the founder of a startup and transitioned from a 30-person company to a team of just 3. As the team got smaller, he found himself more and more engaged with his clients and the value equation. The closer he got to his customers, the more he saw and felt part of the exchange of value.

In 2013, Amanda Palmer spoke at a TED conference about the intimate and unique relationship between an artist and her audience. She talked about fairness, about asking for help, and most importantly about the value exchange. It is hard to understand without standing in someone else's shoes what value a particular thing has to him or her. Yet in practice, we use this narrow definition all day every day. Go to the grocery store, Target, or especially Amazon and immediately you can see that everything has a price. We call that price value.

But here in the world of independent working, value begins to be defined in a whole new way. In Chapter 9, we talked about that messy and tricky art of setting rates—applying value to your time and your work. Here at the lunch table, though, we were talking about a different value exchange—the value of a network.

In a large organization, it seems like there is a full-time job for every minute aspect of the business. There is not just one person in the marketing department, but many. In addition, each has a specific, measurable, and unique role within the team. There are managers and coordinators, writers and social media experts. There are strategists, designers, and technicians. As the business gets smaller, as Michael experienced, the roles become broader. In a 30-person company, the "marketing person" might have to be the strategist and the technician, the writer and the social media coordinator, and sometimes even the designer as well.

But as the company shrinks still further, those mechanics cease to apply. You cannot be, as an army of one, good at everything.

While most people who talk about networking approach it as a tool to find clients and work, I want to look at it through a different lens. A network serves three main purposes for independent professionals, and the sales and business development process is only one of those three—arguably the least effective from a process perspective. If you go out and seek to build your network only to produce income for yourself, you will be what Adam Grant refers to in his book *Give and Take* as the ultimate taker. Certainly, your network will help you get work, but its purpose and value often come from the other two functions.

Your network is an extension of your skill set. As a business operations consultant, I often advise my clients not to put people into roles they either don't like or aren't good at. Dan Sullivan, founder of Strategic Coach, created a framework that is a key to successfully running your own business. It is a continuum of capability ranging from incompetent (the things we are terrible at; for me, this is graphic design) through competent (things we can do but don't enjoy and aren't particularly good at) and excellent (things that we are really good at, enjoy doing, and can do better than most people). The peak of the framework is our unique ability, that thing that each of us does easily, loves to do, brings us great joy and fulfillment, and often provides unique value to others. It is this thing, this unique ability that ideally we should be spending most if not all of our time doing.

But we don't.

We don't because we are so busy doing things that we are incompetent or competent or even excellent at, and this is where your network becomes the most important tool in your arsenal. The very first thing you can and should do is go out and make friends with people who do things at which you are incompetent. Find other independent pros that can fill the gaps in your abilities and hire them. In Chapter 5, we talked about your core team—your attorney, accountant, and insurance agent. These are areas where most of us are either incompetent or competent, but rarely excellent or above, simply because if we were, we would have chosen those fields. If you are an attorney or a CPA, the same advice applies—fill in your gaps by finding and hiring the people who can do the things at which you are incompetent.

The reason for doing this is obvious—you need to do these things, and if you do them yourself you will (a) waste time and (b) do them poorly. However, the secondary reason for quickly shifting these tasks to someone who is good at them is to start a habit that will serve you well in the rest of your professional career. You can't do everything, and if you want to be able to successfully focus on doing the things you do well and get paid for those things, you need to shift as much of the other work that takes up your time off of your own calendar and onto someone else's.

Therefore, your network extends your own abilities—it allows you to accomplish things quickly and efficiently that you couldn't accomplish on your own. In some cases, you may be able to do this for free by bartering your unique ability for someone else's. However, even if you have to pay someone to do these things, it is generally worth it.

The second function of your network, beyond being an extension of your skill set, is for support, for socialization, and for sharing information. In Chapter 2, we talked about the secret life of the self-employed—that rarely discussed group of working professionals that makes up between 10% and 30% of the workforce depending on whose numbers you are looking at. Despite being a substantial percentage of working adults, most freelancers and independent consultants report feeling isolated at times. It is great to roll out of bed and work in your pajamas, but when things are tough, or when you are trying to figure out how to approach a client, or are lacking inspiration, having a strong network can be invaluable.

A strong network is the foundation of a long-term independent career. Your network is the collection of relationships with individuals and organizations that connects you to your customers. While we all tend to build relationships over time, in order to make a successful transition to self-employment, you will need to turn this into an active, consistent process. In this chapter, a number of standard networking practices will be reviewed as well as resources for overcoming some of the hurdles of networking

We understand now that a network is valuable for a variety of reasons, but how do you build a strong network to support you as your business grows? There are three key principles to developing a community of supportive, engaged people who can help you get better at what you do.

1. Meet one person.
2. Help people connect.
3. Don't work alone.

I talked earlier about how many people make the mistake of going into the business card collection process. They go to networking events and talk to 20 or 30 people in one night. They come home with a stack of cards and dutifully record all their connections in a database. They send follow-up emails. They build an enormous, shallow network.

It may feel good to have thousands of contacts in your system, but it won't help if you don't actually know them. So instead of trying to accumulate as many connections as you can, focus on one person at a time. If you go to a big event, don't talk to 20 people, talk to two or three. Find the one person there that you like, that you feel like you could talk to for an hour. Get his or her card, and then call him or her up the next day and schedule a lunch.

While being good at your craft will help you produce good work as a freelancer, nothing will make you as successful as genuinely relating to people. Therefore, once you have connected with someone, your next goal is to help him or her connect with one more person who can help him or her. Over lunch or coffee, ask questions. Resist the temptation to talk about yourself, and instead try to find out about your new friend across the table. Where is he or she in the process? What is tough for him or her right now? What does he or she do best? If you can find a way to help him or her solve a problem, that is great, but the important part is to truly get to know what motivates him or her, why he or she does this work, and where he or she wants to go from there.

One of the best things about working for yourself is the ability to define where and how you work. We talked earlier about the idea of having a personal rhythm—a sense of when we are at our most productive and how much stimulation we need to find an ideal flow of creative energy. However, sometimes we are stuck and isolated because we can work out of our houses. We spend too much time working alone.

While it might feel great to roll out of bed and get a bunch of productive work done before you have taken a shower, working by yourself as a long-term strategy is limiting. You cannot learn new things if you are not interacting with your peers. You will not find new clients if you do not go out and talk to new people. Therefore, the final key to building a strong network is to find ways to work with other people. Not sure how that works? In the next chapter, we will talk about some of the ways to optimize your independent working life, including balancing your work and your life, finding places to work collaboratively, and how to overcome some of the challenges of working independently.

Section III

Strategies for Long-Term Success as an Independent Professional

12

Optimizing Your Independent Career

Between 1992 and 1995, Deion Sanders made professional sports history by becoming one of the only people to play in championship games in two different professional sports. Not two teams, two sports. In 1992, he went to the World Series as an outfielder for the Atlanta Braves. Just two years later, he was playing in the Super Bowl with the San Francisco 49ers.

Sanders' incredible athleticism as well as an insatiable drive for success brought him to the very top of his field—this was a man who knew his strengths. While you may not end up in the football or baseball hall of fame, it is just as important to your career as an independent professional that you understand your talents and actively develop your strengths.

What is talent? When we think about someone who is talented, we often think about someone who has a natural ability to do something. Whether it is the musical talent that allowed Beethoven to perform his first symphony at the age of 7, or the talent for innovation and perfection that made Steve Jobs one of the most successful entrepreneurs in the world, talent can take many forms.

A talent is something you do well, something that comes naturally and easily to you. No one is talented at everything, so the key to success is identifying your own talents. We already learned that a talent is something you can turn into a revenue stream if you package and market it correctly.

But talent alone did not get Deion Sanders to the Super Bowl. Talent needs to be combined with practice in order to become a strength. Time after time as I spoke with freelancers and independent professionals who were successful in making a living over the long term, I found that they had one thing in common: a desire to perfect their craft. They shared their stories about refining their skills, seeking out feedback, and finding ways to get better in order to maximize their ability to leverage their talent to build a successful career.

In 1943, a psychology researcher named Abraham Maslow wrote a paper called "A Theory of Human Motivation." He proposed a theory of a five-stage model that described what humans need to be motivated, to be happy, and to experience the feeling of success. At the bottom layers of the model are the truly basic needs—food, shelter, physical safety, etc. As we move up the model, it is easy to see how work plays into some of these needs. The idea of belonging—being part of something—can be satisfied by family and friends, but is also a big part of the social aspects of work. Higher still we find that we need to feel knowledgeable and competent, and that we are contributing something to the goodness and order of the world.

The final level of Maslow's theory is called Self-Actualization. This is the idea that, at the pinnacle of success, we feel that we are completely fulfilled, both professionally and personally; that we are engaging in a life where we are truly using our talents and following our passions personally and professionally in a truly ideal way. In many cases when I talk to successful independent professionals, they describe a feeling about work and life that matches up quite nicely with Maslow's idea of Self-Actualization.

In Section II, we talked about getting started, getting set up to do business, finding your first client, and making the transition to being a true independent professional. However, once you have made the shift, a new learning cycle begins. You need to figure out how to optimize your ability to earn income and deliver your product efficiently. Here in Section III, we will talk about how to become great at what you do. We will talk about how to make that transition from the lower echelons of the pyramid to the higher, with the goal of achieving the very highest level of success and satisfaction.

Becoming a truly successful freelancer involves striking a balance between three separate but important processes. First, you have to be able to find work. Business development is an integral part of the freelance dance, and requires constant attention if you want to have a steady flow of work. One of the most efficient ways to create a consistent workflow is to build a recognizable personal brand so that you are known in the marketplace as the go-to person for your line of work. That way business will start to come to you. Therefore, in this section we will talk about how to build a brand, and how to refine your talking points about who you are and what you do.

Beyond the challenge of getting work in the first place, you also have to be able to deliver a great result. This means you need to have a thorough understanding of what you do and how you do it, and you need to make sure you are working to keep your skills fresh and relevant. In Section III, we will talk about how to deliver like a pro, and how to handle tricky situations with clients.

Finally, the third factor in succeeding as a free agent over the long haul involves building a balanced life so that you don't feel like a slave to your clients. This means making sure you are taking time for yourself, doing the right work, and thinking about your legacy over the long term.

Balancing work and life means different things to different people. Many independent professionals are working parents who want to be able to control their own schedules and balance work and family. Another emerging trend in freelance work/life balance is the rise of the digital nomad. These are people who have taken the flexibility of freelancing one step further, and leveraged it to allow them to travel and earn money at the same time.

Imagine for a minute that you can work from absolutely anywhere. No need for a desk or an office, no meetings that can't be held over Skype™ or Facetime, no restrictions whatsoever on where you can be physically while you are working. Would you work from home? Or would you choose to travel, leveraging your freedom of movement to explore the world?

Katie Probert chose travel. An avid skier and snowboarder, Katie started her career working in bars because it allowed her to be flexible and free of commitments. She could travel through Europe, spend the skiing season in the Alps, and the summer on the road.

She quickly realized that working the bar scene was a less than fulfilling long-term career. Because she had become fluent in French, Katie realized she could start teaching both French and English as a second language. She also launched a blog and an online business selling hand-made knitted products.

Katie feels like this style of working gives her everything she wants. "Because I now work for myself, I can choose when to work. I want to work in the evenings because I want to snowboard during the day."

One of the reasons Katie has been able to become a digital nomad is her ability to keep her expenses low. It is a common theme among those who choose to travel and work from anywhere—it is not all lattes and fancy resorts. Most digital nomads have crafted their lifestyle to minimize expenses and live in a way that focuses primarily on experiences rather than possessions. Katie says she and her boyfriend struggled initially to find a balance that worked for them, but now they feel like they are right where they want to be.

"Society teaches us to pursue a good job that will eventually lead to owning our own home. Usually this takes a lifetime in a traditional situation, but we decided to change how we lived so that it suited us, and not the other way round. Creating the situation that we're in now required a lot of determination, and was met with a lot of opposition along the way from people who didn't understand what we were doing or why we were doing it. I couldn't imagine until last year how we would make this all work, but we persevered with our hobbies, and eventually got good enough at them that we could earn a living from them."

While many digital nomads are young and often single, without the complications of houses and children, that is not universally true. Quite a few families have chosen to live the digital nomad lifestyle, and have done it successfully.

For Jennifer Miller and her family, the journey started with a decision to spend a year bicycling in Europe. In 2008, Jennifer Miller, her husband and four children sold their house and packed up what was left to spend a year abroad. Six years later, they are still on the road and loving it. I had a chance to talk to Jennifer about the ups and downs of their nomadic life, and how they make it all work.

The roots of Jennifer's wanderlust are firmly planted in the soil of her early life. "I grew up in a family that taught me that my life was NOW, not in ten years or when I became a 'grown up' so I've been encouraged to live fully and pursue my passions from the beginning. I suppose I expected to get married, have kids and travel, because those were the things that had been modeled for me."

While her four kids were very young, Jennifer and her husband Tony felt like having a home and roots in one community made the most sense, but that was a conscious decision and a temporary one. It was never their intent to remain permanently in one place. That said, Jennifer doesn't feel like they were driven to travel the world out of frustration with their lifestyle, but rather that when the time was right they made the transition to traveling because it was what they always wanted to do.

"We have never felt unhappy or unsatisfied with our way of living, in any form of it. There are stages of life, of course, and when our kids were young we chose to stay put, for the most part. We have known, since before we had kids, that big time travel would be a part of their education and upbringing, so it was just a matter of waiting until everyone was out of diapers before moving on to the next adventure. We loved our house in New Hampshire, our community, the work we were doing and our family life. We weren't frustrated at all. We just wanted to pursue another sort of dream."

Transitioning to life on the road is a huge amount of work and represents a daunting risk that many families are unwilling to take. Imagine getting sick in a country where you don't speak the language or running out of money thousands of miles away from the "safety" of where you were born and raised. But for the Millers, the rewards of traveling and experiencing the world as a family far outweighed the worries and risks.

In addition to the worries and risks of the travel itself, Jennifer and Tony were also committed to reducing expenses and creating some revenue streams while they traveled, so that they could prolong the experience as long as possible. Tony, as a software developer, was already well positioned to earn a living while working remotely. Jennifer transitioned from being a teacher to writing full-time. She started a blog to chronicle their family's adventures, and has been a contributing writer for a wide variety of publications.

Writing, software development, web design, and photography are the top professions for digital nomads, and for good reason. In order to make a living while traveling, it is essential to have a work product that can be completed anywhere, and that requires minimal interaction with clients.

The daily routine of digital nomads can vary tremendously. While Katie spends her days skiing and snowboarding, and her evenings writing and teaching, the Millers have their own process. According to Jennifer, "mornings are for work and schooling, afternoons are for adventure. All bets are off if there is an 18-hour bus trip to be made! Tony and I work about 20 hours a week, each, which is about what the kids invest in their required book work (of course they are always learning!)"

Their four kids are homeschooled, so the whole family works and plays together as they travel the globe. To pull this off, one of the things they focus on when choosing locations to stay is Internet access. Most digital nomads work off laptops or mobile phones, and the ability to connect and communicate is critical to their ability to earn money on the road.

The digital nomad lifestyle is clearly not for everyone, but it has become increasingly common as technology and access to cloud services via the Internet have become increasingly available around the globe. For those who choose this path, it is a luxury to be able to combine doing work that they enjoy with living a lifestyle that feels authentic.

These three factors—business development, delivering like a pro, and thinking long term—are the elements that will take your independent work style to the next level, beyond survival and into happiness.

13

Co-Working and Connecting with the New Community of Independent Professionals

Heavy exposed beams span the ceiling, and wide-plank hardwood floors creak underfoot. Light streams into the space from the street level windows that show the steady flow of foot traffic on Atlantic Avenue. Long tables span the open spaces, and are filled with people industriously typing, busily sketching on whiteboards, or engaged in focused dialog over their laptop screens.

This is Workbar—a co-working space in the leather district just a few blocks from the waterfront, and a convenient walk from Boston's South Station. There is a hum of activity in the space—subdued because the people who work here know that in an open space, sound travels quickly. People are seated at the tables or on high stools at counters, sitting side by side but mostly working independently.

Bill Jacobson founded Workbar, and it is his vision of a shared workspace that has driven everything about this space from the layout of different working areas (a place for people who want quiet, a place that feels like a coffee shop, a place for people who are doing phone and video calls with many tiny, individuals rooms) to the social sharing of photos and interests that make the space feel friendly and personal. For Bill, the idea of co-working is all about creating connections.

One of the most important tools in a freelancer's kit is the ability to keep fixed costs low while leveraging the look and feel of an office when needed. However, co-working goes beyond the ability to host a meeting or publish an address; it is about becoming part of a community. In the last 10 years as more professionals have moved into freelancing, systems and support structures have emerged to facilitate their unique needs.

While shared office spaces have existed for many years in the form of executive suites, co-working is quite a different idea. Executive suites and shared offices typically offer a receptionist, a mailbox, and the ability to utilize conference rooms and shared services such as copiers. What sets co-working apart and makes it so much more valuable to freelancers is the conscious effort to connect the individuals who are sharing space. Shared executive offices tend to be long hallways filled with private office suites where residents work behind closed doors. Co-working spaces, by contrast, are often open spaces where people can work side by side. Most co-working spaces include a selection of public and private spaces, and typically provide telephone booths or other small private spaces for phone calls, leaving most work to be done in the more open spaces.

This contrast creates a world of difference in terms of the atmosphere and the culture. Co-working spaces host cocktail parties, hackathons, meetups, and other events designed to help members get to know one another, and to leverage the collective membership's connections to the outside world. There are boards or other visuals to show who is working on what, and to help people make introductions and get to know one another. There is a deliberate effort to make the workspace feel like a shared resource that is alive with activity.

As we walked through the various areas at Workbar, Bill talked about the variety of different people who are coming to co-working, and the strong demand they have seen in the last few years. He describes their population as about evenly split into three different types of users: freelancers, small startup companies, and employees whose home offices are not located locally.

Each of these groups has a bit of a different reason for being attracted to a place like Workbar. Freelancers tend to be interested in the connections they can make, the sense of community, and the ability to have a professional space for meetings. In their 2013 survey, Deskmag found that 71% of freelancers reported feeling more creative since joining a co-working space, and 90% were more self-confident.

Entrepreneurs come to co-working spaces for slightly different reasons. First on the list is flexibility. In startup mode, startup founders love the ability to have more or less space as needed, and to know they are not locked into a long-term lease. In addition, many co-working spaces are also home to accelerators or incubators, which act as catalysts to help connect startups with funding and mentors, and provide support for their success. Finally, it is a great way to find freelancers who can do piece work such as marketing and branding.

Co-working arose as a trend around the mid to late 1990s. The name was coined by Bernard DeKoven, a former teacher turned video game programmer, who used it to describe an environment that would "facilitate collaborative work and business meetings, coordinated by computers." DeKoven saw the potential to leverage the connections that professionals have in a face-to-face way, as well as with technology. He published his ideas in a mini-book called *Connected Executives*, and then launched a website around these ideas that continues to exist today as The Co-working Institute.

Since those early days, the trend has caught on and grown rapidly. The idea that independent professionals could, for a small price, have access not only to a professional space to meet with clients, but also to leverage the resources and connections of other freelancers was quickly embraced. By the beginning of 2013, there were over 100,000 professionals working in co-working spaces around the world according to the Global Co-working Survey.

What is it about co-working that is drawing in so many professionals? As we talked about in Chapter 1, one of the major driving factors in the popularity of co-working is the simple increase in the number of people who are freelancing. As the population of independent workers has grown, so have their needs for collaborative space, and their needs to grow their networks to feed the business development pipeline.

While independent workers are not tracked in a separate category by the Bureau of Labor Statistics, a variety of independent surveys have marked the rapid growth of both jobs and workers in the freelance category. Elance—a major marketplace for freelancers—saw 51% growth in the number of jobs posted on their boards in 2013. While their survey suggests that approximately one-third of the current U.S. workforce is comprised of freelancers, projected growth indicates that by 2020 there will be nearly an equal number of employees as freelancers. Genesis Research found that 72% of current employees expressed a strong desire to shift to being independent workers, and that the trend was increasingly pronounced in the Millennial generation. Finally, Intuit's 2020 trends report found that "more than 80% of large corporations plan to substantially increase their use of a flexible workforce in the coming years."

The continued strong growth of co-working clearly reflects the growing numbers of people who are working independently, but what benefits does co-working offer that make it worthwhile for freelancers (many of whom work hard to minimize their fixed expenses) to pay for the cost of a desk and choose voluntarily to work in an office environment? Some of the biggest benefits of co-working go far beyond a simple need for space.

- Conference Rooms—One of the main reasons that freelancers are drawn to co-working spaces is the ability to reserve and use professional conference room space with presentation facilities. Trying to land a big client while shouting over the milk steamer at your local coffee house can be the death of a promising business opportunity. Being able to deliver a great sales pitch in a professional environment is a huge asset and well worth the cost of a basic membership.
- Physical Address—Another big giveaway about the size of your business is your address. If you are putting a PO Box on your business cards or your website, you are declaring that your operation is too small to have an office. Co-working spaces allow tenants to list the space address as their own, which can be a big advantage in boosting your business image. It also allows you to avoid using your home address in publicly accessible documents.
- Networking—Freelancers must spend a percentage of their time actively delivering their services in order to generate revenue. While some independent workers make a living through subscription services or other recurring revenue sources, most are still trading hours for dollars. Co-working creates an opportunity to work and network at the same time. Since co-working spaces tend to be small and have a heavy focus on community, it is common and logical for co-working "neighbors" to refer business to one another. In addition, most co-working spaces host "jellies" or other events, which draw members of the surrounding community into the space, which further extends the networking benefits of being part of the environment.
- Extended Capabilities—Many business opportunities arise out of consulting engagements. If I am working with an organization on its strategy, and I see that marketing is a weak point, the first thing I will want to do is recommend that the organization engage a resource to improve its marketing capabilities. If I am not a marketing expert (and I'm not), I will refer the organization to someone I know and trust to ensure that it gets the best results. Co-working creates a simple and logical process to extend my own capabilities.

- Office Hours and Partners—Quite a few co-working spaces are also home to accelerators and incubators. It is a natural partnership and even if you aren't part of the accelerator you can often sign up for time with mentors and other sponsors who hold office hours within the space. It is a great way to connect with resources who can answer your questions about legal issues, HR concerns, taxes, and corporate structure. While you will need to engage with some of the professionals who offer office hours on a more formal basis if you need more than just a question answered, it is a good way to meet reputable service providers and have a go-to resource for your business needs.

It is true that most co-working spaces will provide most or all of these services and benefits, but as the number of co-working spaces grows, there has been a trend toward differentiation and specialization. Some focus on a specific industry while others look to provide services that are of specific value to entrepreneurs vs. freelancers or vice versa. A very small number of co-working chains or franchises exist, but most spaces are single site endeavors launched by entrepreneurs who have a strong connection to the local community and economy. In fact, for many founders of co-working spaces, it was out of a desire to have access to such a space for their own businesses that they got involved as the founder.

As Bill walks us through Workbar, he highlights the unique architecture and modern plan of the working spaces. The intent, he says, is to create a space that feels productive and stimulating. The design of Workbar is intentional and bears almost no resemblance to a traditional office. This is in part to combat the question many people ask when considering co-working—why would I want to go back to working in an office when I worked so hard to get away from that environment? The idea of cubicles is anathema to entrepreneurs and freelancers, and as such most co-working spaces, if they offer cubicle space, refer to it as desk space or rented desks, and use low walled or no-wall options in order to prevent the environment from looking like a scene from "Dilbert."

There are other ways that co-working spaces set themselves apart from traditional working environments. In many cases, they operate more like incubators or even schools, offering entrepreneurs and freelancers opportunities to add to their own skill sets. Several types of adjacent organizations are often found in partnership with or directly run by the same organizations that operate the space itself.

- Accelerators—Since many of the people who are drawn to working in shared spaces are entrepreneurs, it follows that angel investors and funders see these spaces as an opportunity to find new ventures to fund, and even to host cohorts of their own accelerators.
- Training Schools—General Assembly, which started in New York City and has expanded to a variety of locations around the United States, launched as a startup school offering courses in entrepreneurship, programming, and other skills that startups often need. Many other co-working spaces host courses and topics of interest to their memberships, either as part of their services or in partnership with organizations that offer training.
- Industry Focus—While many co-working spaces will host entrepreneurs and freelancers from any line of work, some are specifically focused on one vertical. Boston is home to LearnLaunch—a unique entrepreneurship campus and affiliated accelerator that hosts only startups and entrepreneurs working in the education technology space. Down the street is Space with a Soul, which is home to a variety of individuals and small companies that work for social good.

The acceleration and differentiation of co-working spaces is happening at an astonishing pace. Between 2005 (when the first co-working space was launched) and 2013, the number of spaces in the United States offering co-working grew from 1 to 781. In addition, the growth is still strong, with 83% growth in the number of spaces between 2012 and 2013, and 117% growth in the number of memberships in that same timeframe.

As we finish our tour of the space, Bill Jacobsen heads back to his office to work on his expansion plans. The continued growth of freelancing, as well as the robust startup community, means that for now, his biggest problem is having enough space to meet the demand.

For independent professionals, the growth of facilities that offer services to improve productivity, build community, and facilitate networking is great news. These spaces have eliminated several major obstacles to successfully working for yourself: space, community, and the ability to easily network with others in the field.

Being part of a community is a huge benefit for a free agent, but sometimes it can feel like a lot of pressure. After all, if there are so many other independent professionals working in co-working spaces, doesn't that mean there is a lot of competition? It does, but fortunately, the market is big enough for many people to be successful. All you need to do is know how to stand out. In the next chapter, we will talk about how to leverage what is unique about you, so you can find the right clients to keep you busy and happy doing the work you love.

14

Building a Brand

When you are successful in building your independent business, you start to see patterns in the work that you do. These patterns show where and how you do your best work, and that reputation is how you start to develop something called a brand. As you develop a longer-term client base, this brand is something you will want to develop actively, defining a clear niche, and developing your authority within that niche. This is a critical step in getting a steady stream of ongoing business.

We hear a lot about branding these days, but what is a brand, really? Is it a logo? Is it what you do? Is it what people think you do? The reality is a combination of all of those elements.

The basic structure of a brand includes your company name, logo, and tagline. However, over the long term the brand identity becomes something much more. It becomes the perception of your organization in the marketplace. Let's start by looking at some of the most famous brands in the world of big business to see how this works.

In 1977, Mike Markkula became a partner with Steve Jobs and Steve Wozniak in their emerging business, Apple Computer Corporation. Today, we know Apple as one of the most recognized brands in the world, but at the time, with its rainbow logo and new fangled ideas about personal technology, Apple had not yet made its mark on the world. It was in those early days that Markkula, an investor and marketing savant, wrote a three-point plan for how Apple would focus its efforts as it developed a relationship with its customers. His points were as follows:

1. Empathy—We will truly understand their needs better than any other company.
2. Focus—In order to do a good job of those things we decide to do, we must eliminate all of the unimportant opportunities.

3. Impute—People do judge a book by its cover. We may have the best product, the highest quality, the most useful software, etc.; if we present them in a slipshod manner, they will be perceived as slipshod. If we present them in a creative, professional manner, we will impute the desired qualities.

These three points drove the development of the Apple brand because they clearly defined what the company was and what it was not. Thus, even when the tagline, the logo, or even the primary product that Apple produced changed significantly, customers still recognized the qualities underpinning the brand and continued to buy its products.

So what about you? Do you think you are too small to think of your brand the way Apple does? You are not—in fact, the very best thing you can do for yourself is to spend some time developing a clear and specific understanding of how you create unique value for your customers.

We live in a world where, for better or for worse, we are bombarded on a daily basis with advertising messages. A Japanese soft drink company is working on sending its product to the moon so it can be there to proactively quench the thirst of future astronauts. American consumers are, whether they know it or not, some of the most educated buyers in the world. We expect every organization that wants a piece of our hard earned income to be able to articulate not only what they will do, but why they are uniquely perfect beyond every other competitor out there to give us what we need.

Because the Internet has given free agents the ability to have an online presence, we can be compared side by side with large organizations with substantially deeper pockets for advertising and marketing revenue. On the one hand, this can be daunting. How can we possibly compete with multi-million or even billion dollar brands? However, the basics of branding are quite simple, and in fact are critical for us to define even if we never venture into the world of advertising. Why? Because branding is all about clearly articulating who you are so that your ideal customers know that you are perfect for them.

In the wide world of potential clients, as an individual, there is no possibility that you will be able to provide service to even a minute percentage of the people who need what you offer. There simply isn't enough time in the day. However, as an independent professional, you only need a select few. There are two ways to go about building awareness so your potential customers can find you and you can have a chance to write a proposal. The first is the fire hose option. It works like this:

1. Write a generic description of your services (including contact info).
2. Pop it onto a postcard template.
3. Buy a list of 1,000 businesses in your region.
4. Mail the postcard and wait for the phone to ring.

Of those 1,000 cards, 100 of them will be returned to you as businesses have moved or closed. Another 850 of them will go straight into the trash. The remaining 10 to 50 will get passed along, briefly read, and, if you are truly lucky, a few people will take the time to look at your website or pick up the phone.

The average response for a mass mailing of this type is .5% to 2%, which means that you should get 5 to 20 phone calls from your campaign and of those maybe 1 to 5 will be interested in buying something. So, if the whole deal cost you $1,000 to put together (including design, cost of cards, cost of postage, cost of the list, etc.), you will hopefully get one client out of the deal. Depending on how much each client earns you, this might be worth the investment.

The reason the return rate is so low on the fire hose approach is our overall saturation with marketing materials and junk mail. The Internet often feels like a huge roomful of people all running past you shouting about whatever it is they are trying to sell. It is exhausting right up until you are the one who wants people to buy things from you. Then you wish the whole world would stop and pay attention.

So back to branding and why it is important—a brand is what will help you capture the attention of, if not the whole world, at least the people who are highly likely to want to buy something from you. In addition, this is the secret to developing a good brand: know your customer. Remember point 1 on Apple's marketing vision—understand your customer better than anyone.

The best way to do that is to go out and conduct interviews. Through your local library (or online if you have a library card number handy) you can access a tool called referenceUSA, which will allow you to search for companies by size, type, location, and a variety of other metrics. This is a great way to find companies that you can help.

What's that? You don't know what size or type company you want to sell your services to? Well that is a good place to start. In Chapter 6 when we talked about developing revenue from talent, we talked about finding something you do that has value to someone else (usually a business, but not always). As you think about the value you provide, it is likely that it applies to a specific type or size of company. For example, big companies are likely to have the resources to hire their own graphic designers. However, a small company of 20 to 100 people might not have the resources to have someone on staff.

Knowing what type or industry you should target may have more to do with your background and experience than anything else may. In 2010, I received a call from an advertising agency in Boston. It had found me through my book and my website, and wanted me to come in and talk to its employees about providing management training to its up and coming leaders. It seemed like a perfect fit, until it asked me for another advertising firm as a reference. I told the agency that I could provide it with quite a few happy clients to call, but unfortunately, none of them was in advertising. That was the end of the deal—I didn't have direct ad agency experience, so no matter how qualified I was, the agency wouldn't hire me.

There are a few industries where this is the case. Venture capital firms and financial services companies often operate the same way. If they don't have someone in their inner circle who has already worked with you, they won't do business with you. However, the reverse is true and can work well in your favor. If you have strong connections in a particular industry, it can be a great way to build a niche. If you are a management expert who has worked with a couple of ad agencies, you can tell your prospective clients that you are the best fit because you know their industry. Learn some of the language, some of the hot buttons, and some of the influencers, and the next thing you know, you have a steady stream of clients.

Building a brand is about finding and defining what is unique about you and your services. The first step is knowing what those unique elements are. The next is translating them into some tangible materials to use in marketing your business.

Logo—A logo is a unique visual representation of your name and tagline that you can put on business cards, letterhead, and other materials. While there are some tools and resources that can help you create a logo online for not much money, this is definitely a time to leverage your network and get a designer to help you. Your logo is going to be the single most visible part of your business to potential clients. It will be on every business card and every communication you have, so it needs to look professional, and ideally, it needs to help you convey why your clients should work with you. That is a lot of work for a small piece of art to accomplish, and having a designer help you with it will mean that you feel confident about every card you hand out and every proposal you send.

Tagline—This is often part of your logo, and is a few sentences that describe the core value of your business. Think of some famous tag lines and you can see right away that something about the brand is being conveyed. Snapple, for example, uses "made from the best stuff on earth" as their tagline. That short sentence is designed to make you feel good about buying and drinking their product. Staples, the office supply giant, focuses all of their branding around the idea of being "easy." Why is easy important? Because its customers are busy business people who don't have time for things that are hard and complicated. Therefore, when you are thinking about a tagline, think about what problem you solve for your clients, what unique ability you have to help your customers be successful.

Social Media—In addition to a logo and a website, most independent professionals maintain a website with a blog, and are active on social media. The Internet, in general, and social media tools like LinkedIn, Twitter, Facebook, and others are ways for you to convey more detail about yourself, your business, and your brand. It is where you can tell your story. There are books written about how to leverage social media for business growth, so for now we will stick to the basics. To effectively leverage social media to spread the word about your brand, you need to do a few things. First, you need to reserve your business name on as many of these outlets as you can. If your name is common or overlaps with a big player in the corporate world, this can be a challenge. As we discussed earlier, picking a unique business name is an important part of setting up your business. However, even if you can't have your first choice, sign up for all of the major social media services using the same name so that no one else can take it.

Once you have your name set up, populate each page with your logo and tagline, as well as contact information and a link back to your web page. That is the easy part. The hard part about social media is knowing what to say, when to say it, and offering something of value so people will follow you and share your updates. To do that successfully, you will need a strategy.

Once you have established a beachhead for your brand in terms of a web presence and basic social media capabilities, you are ready to start delivering your value message to the world.

15

Delivering a Great Result

Imagine for a minute that you are an executive—a business owner whose profits or losses will come in part because of the decisions you make every day. It shouldn't be a big stretch; those of us who are independent professionals are, for all intents and purposes, business owners. However, for this example, let's imagine that you are running a larger organization, say 200 employees and $100 million in revenue. Your company, Wilson's Widgets, is coming out with a new product and you want to figure out how to get the word out to your customers about this great new tool. Wilson's Widgets competes with Spacely Sprockets and you want to make sure that not only your own customers know about your great advance in widget development, but you would love to attract some of Spacely's customers, too. Your sales and marketing team knows that you have made a big investment and retooled 50% of your factory to produce your great new invention, so when your vice president of marketing approaches you and suggests hiring a consultant to help develop the marketing plan, you say, "Of course."

This is the moment that independent professionals get the call and an opportunity to come in and pitch. Most of the time we think about the proposal process from our point of view—we spend time networking and meeting people, we do great work, we bill our time and pay our taxes and worry about whether we have the right insurance coverage. We think about how to schedule our clients and what tools we will need to produce what we have been asked to make. However, let's take a minute and try to think about an ideal engagement from the perspective of the client.

You are back in the CEO chair at Wilson's Widgets and today you are going to meet with a marketing consultant who came highly recommended from several colleagues. There is a lot riding on this project and you want to make sure you pick the right person who is going to be able to handle the whole project, be creative and insightful, and work well with everyone on your team.

When the consultant candidate walks in the door, what are you looking for? Most likely, you will want to see some of the following things.

Look and act like a professional. One of the most important characteristics you can cultivate when you are working for yourself is a strong, professional persona. Most independent professionals, regardless of their specific area of expertise, are being hired as experts. That means you need to look and sound the part. There are several elements to looking like a professional, and the first and most obvious is dress.

While it is possible to walk into a startup and find an environment full of people in jeans and t-shirts, that doesn't mean you should expect that, so dress accordingly. The rule of thumb for dress code is always one step above what you expect your client to be wearing. However, for an initial meeting, it is best to err on the side of being overdressed.

If you aren't sure what constitutes professional dress, your best bet is to get some help. All of us have someone in our contact list that has a sense of professional style. If you don't (and I personally don't), it is a good idea to reach out to that friend and have him or her help you curate your wardrobe. You don't need to spend thousands of dollars on a professional clothing collection, but you do need one or two go-to outfits that help you make the right impression.

Acting like a professional goes beyond clothing. Here are some key elements that I would expect of any independent professional in the first meeting.

Do your homework—If you are going to meet with a client for the first time, find out everything you can about them. How long have they been in business? Who are their competitors? What do they make? LinkedIn can be a huge help when you are trying to find the inside scoop on a company. If your network is big enough, you may know someone who works there. The more you can find out before you walk in the door, the more you can anticipate what will help you win the business.

Bring business cards—I am always surprised when I meet someone professionally and they don't have a card. While technology has come a long way in terms of keeping us connected, the fact is that if I don't walk away from our first meeting with your card in my hand, I may not remember to connect with you on social media later. Since you can get a box of business cards for about $20, there is really no excuse to skip this step.

Polish your pitch—No one likes to sit through a rambling version of the story of your life. You may only have a few minutes to capture the attention and convince the decision maker that you are the right person for the job. That means you need to be prepared to talk clearly, articulately, and concisely about who you are, what you do, and how you do it. Be ready for questions about how big your company is, and how often you have worked with companies like the one you are pitching. In order to convince someone that he or she should hire you, you have to demonstrate that you are the right person for the job. This may mean altering your pitch a little based on the client needs.

Ask questions—This initial meeting is your time to ask all the questions you have about the nature of the project. While talking about yourself and your capabilities is one way to demonstrate that you are a good fit for a job, asking great questions is an even better way. As you seek to understand every aspect of the client's needs, it will give the client the impression that you are customizing your proposal just for them, and that you are truly interested in understanding what they are looking for.

Be mindful of time—It is a good idea to ask how long you have at the beginning of your pitch meeting. If you have just a few minutes, you will want to approach the meeting differently than if you have an hour. While some businesspeople feel comfortable running over on time during a meeting, it is a good idea to keep your eye on the clock and wrap things up a few minutes before the scheduled end of the meeting. This helps set the tone that you are respectful of their time, and I hope that will help them do the same.

Mind your manners—While you might eventually get to a point with a client where you can be casual, the first meeting is not that moment. It is natural to talk a bit about yourself, maybe talk about sports, your kids, or your hobbies. The client is going to want to get to know you as a person before it decides to engage with you on a project. However, be sure to keep these conversations high level and professional.

Once you have set a professional tone with your appearance and your approach to the meeting, and you have followed the steps in Part 2 to write a great proposal and get a signed contract for the work, then it is time to deliver a great result for your client. If you have successfully started the engagement off on a positive and professional note, the next step is to kick off the project and manage it through to completion.

There are books, courses, and even certifications that detail all of the elements of effective project management. I won't try to duplicate all of that information here, but if you have come into freelancing without a strong grounding in project management, I strongly recommend that you take a course or read some of the great books out there on the subject. For the purposes of this conversation, we will focus on some of the aspects of project management that are unique to working independently.

The first and most important part of delivering great results involves setting clear expectations. This is a layered process that begins by asking good questions in the initial meeting with your client, and continues on through your proposal and your scope of work. You should be quite specific about things like timeframes, deliverables, what you need the client to provide, and any other critical requirements.

As part of setting expectations, it is a good idea to create a schedule that outlines where and when the work will be done. If there are collaborative elements where you will need time from your client or a member of its team, make sure you get those meetings on the calendar as early as possible. The schedule exists both to communicate the process to everyone involved, and to keep everyone accountable to a timeframe. The schedule should force both you and your client to think realistically about turnaround times, and should be created with 10% to 20% extra time to account for any issues or delays.

The schedule (and any changes) should be included as part of a weekly summary communication you send to your client, giving it an update of what is complete, what is still to come, and what (if anything) is holding up the process. Both the schedule and a regular routine of check-in conversations should give you the tools and structure you need to manage expectations if things start to go off course.

Beyond the structure of an engagement, and the general tenets of professionalism, as an independent professional you are also expected to behave a bit differently than an internal employee. Being a great consultant is different from being a great employee. You are being paid for your expertise, as well as your ability to help your client understand how to integrate your recommendations.

To add real value, there are several elements that most successful consultants have in common.

Have an opinion—When I was first getting started as an IT consultant, I attended a client meeting with one of the senior people on our team. In the meeting, we were asked whether they should invest in a new server or whether they should consider moving to the "Cloud." At the time, cloud services were a relatively new phenomenon, and many of our clients were struggling with this same decision. The senior consultant talked for a few minutes about the pros and cons of each option, and at the end made a strong recommendation against buying a new server. The main difference between a consultant and a counselor is that a counselor helps you consider the relevant information, but leaves the ultimate decision up to you. A consultant is paid not only to give you all of the information about a particular decision, but also to make a recommendation based on that information.

Be practical—Theory and practice are two different things. While we often think about things in the abstract, when it comes to giving advice or providing a service to a client, it is very important to consider the actual facts of the individual situation. While it made complete sense for this particular client to move toward the cloud, we did not make that recommendation to every client.

Be passionate—Most great freelancers choose their field of expertise because they have both a passion and a talent for that work. Having a level of enthusiasm for the work that you do is important, and bringing a level of positive energy to an engagement is a good thing. However, beyond being passionate about your subject matter, you need to be passionate about your client's success. Let's take an example. Noelle is a graphic designer who builds beautiful websites. She loves artistic designs, and enjoys the challenge of creating something that is just right for her clients. When she engages with clients, she gives them the choice of either a template-based design or something she builds from scratch. If she had the choice, she would build every site from scratch, but she knows that it usually adds significantly to the cost to do so. So rather than pitching every client the perfect solution, she gives them the option to save some time and money. That is a perfect synthesis of passion for the work and passion for the client.

Be thick-skinned—Not everyone is going to love everything you do. When you spend hours developing a solution to a particular client's problem, it can be pretty deflating when it is met with a lukewarm response. While it would be nice if all feedback were offered in a constructive and positive way, it doesn't always happen that way. Your focus should always be on getting the client what it needs, and that means having thick skin and pushing forward until you find the answer that works.

Understand the business perspective—Almost all of the work that freelancers are hired to do has some connection to a business need. It is very rare that a company will pay good money for a project that doesn't have any business value. Because of that, solutions should always be crafted with the business perspective in mind. While businesses vary in their goals, most initiatives fall into one of three categories. So, whenever you are working on a project, ask yourself how you are (1) attracting new customers, (2) keeping existing customers happy, and (3) making the company more efficient. Alternatively, remember the three Rs of Recruitment, Retention, and Revenue.

Be resourceful—Sometimes you just can't do something the way it should be done. Most organizations don't have an unlimited budget, so while the perfect solution might not be within their reach, a great consultant will help find ways to get as close to the ideal as possible. To do this you need to think outside the box.

The best client relationships happen when you can bring your unique abilities to bear on a problem that a company or an individual has not been able to solve. While it is ideal to create a long-term relationship with every client, there are some times when you are just there to solve a single problem. However, ideally if you do it well, it will lead to more business through referrals or repeat business.

These long-term relationships are built on one thing—trust. David Maister, author of *The Trusted Advisor*, lists trust as the single most important factor in building a strong and successful client relationship. Trust is at the core of every productive relationship between an independent professional and his or her client. If you are focused on doing the right thing for your customer, you will never lack for clients.

16

Balancing Independent Work and Life

In the summer of 2007, Penelope Trunk was the image of a successful businesswoman. Living in New York City, an entrepreneur and veteran of three startups, Penelope was at the very top of the game. She worked 80+ hours a week, engaging two nannies to provide round the clock childcare for her two children—a refrain that is all too common as women attempt to balance a high-paying, high-powered job with the needs of their families. Penelope, like Sheryl Sandberg, had created a life that revolved around one thing—work. But when she was faced with a huge upheaval in her life that ultimately culminated in divorce, she had to make a big change.

So, she packed up her kids and moved to Wisconsin.

Penelope is the first to admit that she had no desire to be a stay-at-home mother, and in fact, her primary goal in making this massive geographic shift was financial.

"To do a startup and be the breadwinner when you're a single parent is nearly impossible—I don't think you will find another woman who has done that so I knew I couldn't do it in New York City because of the cost of living."

Faced with an unacceptable schedule, combined with an outrageous cost of living, Penelope Trunk moved out of New York City. She cut her cost of living by a substantial margin by relocating, and was able to leverage technology to stay in the game by becoming a free agent.

Today, Penelope's life bears no resemblance to her former career in the city. She starts her days cooking breakfast with eggs laid by the chickens she feeds herself. Instead of sitting in board meetings and firing off emails, she weeds her garden and drives her kids to music lessons. Does she work? Absolutely, but she does it on her terms. She takes on coaching clients, provides career advice via her blog, and finds ways to promote her book, all from a small farm in the western corner of Wisconsin.

While her goal was to balance her budget, what she found after the transition was that she had changed the balance of her life as well. Her shift to freelancing, and her subsequent transition to life on a farm, completely changed her schedule and her approach to work.

Technology has blurred the lines between work and home. It is the tool that allowed Penelope to make the shift away from an untenable schedule and to leverage a lower cost of living in order to live the life she wanted to live. But technology is a double edged sword—if you can work anywhere anytime, how do you unwind? How do you get away from the office when the office is your home?

This is a challenge that is particularly tough for freelancers, not only because we can work from our homes, but also because for most of us, the business is highly dependent on our own efforts. If we stop looking for new business, and if we stop doing work, even for a small period of time, the revenue stops flowing and the business grinds to a halt.

As you first get your free agent career off the ground, it is a constant struggle to get clients. As your business grows and becomes more successful, you may find that business comes to you through referrals, even when you are not out looking for it every day. In the course of the ebb and flow of work, you will have busy times and less busy times. The trick to balancing your work and your life comes down to five essential habits.

REST AND RECHARGE

Having a Smartphone, a tablet, a laptop, and all of the other tools of the trade make it incredibly easy to work anytime, anywhere. However, it comes with a real and somewhat insidious downside. If you never stop working, you burn out, and you become incredibly inefficient and unproductive. In fact, research has shown that spending more time with our technology causes us to have trouble relating to people in the real world. (MIT professor Sherry Turkle makes the case in her 2011 book *Alone Together: Why We Expect More from Technology and Less from Each Other.*)

Most people, if you ask them, will tell you that staying connected all the time is stressful. Yet even on vacation, people continue to stay connected. A whopping 83% of travelers planned to stay connected on vacation according to an American Express survey, and another 64% planned to check their work email every day! We feel like we have to stay on top of everything all the time, especially free agents who are often the only face of the company. Failing to respond to a client for a week or more can be deadly, so instead of proactively communicating to our clients that we will be away, or making contingency plans so someone will respond to a crisis, we simply keep checking our email.

But that little habit is truly terrible for our brains. Nicholas Carr, author of *The Shallows: What the Internet is Doing to Our Brains*, is one of the many modern voices suggesting that constant connectivity leads to shallow interpersonal connections, stress, anxiety, and overall unhappiness. If we can't turn away from work for even a day, we put ourselves at risk of being profoundly unhappy both in work and in life.

Getting into the habit of turning off your work email on your phone over the weekend is a good place to start. While some of us do get client emails on Saturdays and Sundays, most working people don't expect a response until Monday. Therefore, while you may miss the occasional missive, for the most part there will be little or no impact on your business. Moreover, beyond turning off your technology, it is good to get into the habit of taking a break from work completely if you can. While it is tempting to take the time to do a little work here and there, failing to give your brain a chance to disconnect means missing out on an opportunity to recharge in a small way every week. Those small rests lead to more efficient work and more productivity.

CONNECT WITH OTHER INDEPENDENT PROFESSIONALS

We have talked at length in this book about the lack of formal training and recognition around the free agent career path. We don't teach our kids how to run their own businesses in school, we don't talk about the freelance workforce in the labor market numbers, and there is simply not enough information and support from the education system on how to be a successful freelancer. That lack, combined with the fact that many freelancers work out of their houses, leads to a sense of isolation and a lack of knowledge sharing that can be incredibly discouraging.

Finding a community of free agents is one of the best things you can do to support yourself on this career path. Whether you do it through a meet up (start one if there isn't one in your area) or through a co-working community, or simply meeting with friends who also work independently, make the time to connect regularly with other professionals. These people can offer guidance and support when things are tough, and can celebrate with you when you have a win.

In addition to being a supportive community, a network of other independent professionals has the potential to become a consortium where you can share work, and even cover for one another for vacations or when things get busy.

KEEP IMPROVING YOUR TECHNIQUE

Many people who decide to work for themselves, whether it is becoming a marketing consultant or opening a bakery, do so because they have a passion for the craft. It might be enough for an employee to merely be good at his or her job if he or she can earn a living doing it. However, to want to invest the time and effort required into managing your own business, you need to have passion for your work. One of the things that sustain passion over time is the ability to learn new techniques and to get better at what you do, and this generally comes from investing time in professional development.

Professional development comes in a variety of flavors and forms. It can be formal training such as pursuing a master's degree, or it can be more informal, such as working with a mentor. However, whatever the approach, keeping your skills fresh and rekindling your love of the work is an important part of maintaining balance in your work.

As consultants, we often feel the pressure of trying to get as many hours of client work onto our schedules as we can. However, in doing so we sometimes create a grind that undermines our enjoyment. No one likes to do a mediocre job at something they truly enjoy, and so when we push too hard to fit in many clients, we sometimes don't give ourselves enough time to do a great and satisfying job.

The balancing act of making time for self-improvement includes both finding opportunities to learn new and better ways of working and allowing enough time in your own schedule to be able to be innovative and creative. Often trying a new technique means being a little inefficient as you get used to a new way of doing something.

MAKE TIME FOR FAMILY

One of the challenges that face both independent professionals and employees alike in terms of managing a balance between home and work is the issue of childcare. While many freelancers opt for traditional methods such as daycare or nannies, one of the benefits of a flexible schedule is the ability to spend more time at home rather than being tied to the office. With that said, juggling childcare and trying to work at the same time rarely works. Earlier this year, I spoke with Pamela Price, author of *How to Work and Homeschool*, to learn more about how she juggles her freelance career and her family.

Standing on her front porch, Pamela Price can see the acceleration of homeschooling happening right in front of her eyes. "We homeschool, my next door neighbors homeschool, the family two doors down are going to start homeschooling a middle schooler. It's happening everywhere. I know people who are either doing it right now, have done it, or have seriously contemplated it. It's like a homeschooling laboratory."

Accelerating at a pace that many CEOs dream of for their corporations, homeschooling is the fastest-growing form of education in America. From 1999 to 2007, the number of homeschooled students increased by 74% according to the National Center for Education Statistics (2007 is the most recent data they have) and now includes about 4% of school-aged kids in the United States. A practice that was once considered a fringe activity by a few extremists is now a mainstream method of education with support groups, technology resources, consultants, books, and myriad other products all targeting this growing demographic of learners.

Pamela Price and her husband were already sure they would homeschool their son through preschool when their choice was solidified by a reaction to peanuts. The whole landscape of her son's safety changed in an instant. When choosing a preschool became not only about trying to find the level of program quality they were looking for, but also about scrutinizing allergy policies, Pamela and her husband felt the homeschool option was the best choice for their family.

Living in the epicenter of the homeschool movement, Pamela is the author of *How to Work and Homeschool*. She has observed both the increase in parents considering homeschooling and the changing perception of school administrators about kids whom homeschool. She realized that a tipping point had been reached in the acceptance of homeschooling when she ran into the principal of a school district that they had considered moving into years earlier. When the principal asked how things were going and Pamela revealed that they were homeschooling, she found an unexpected ally.

"She turned to me and said, 'You made your best possible choice.' She said, 'I know him, I know what you're doing, and you're fine.' I didn't realize how much I needed to hear that. Looking forward, if we already have principals at the elementary level who are not recoiling in horror from the idea of homeschooling, then who knows what's possible down the road?"

In fact, Pamela's approach to education most closely resembles an entrepreneurship model where she and her son decide what learning experiences they want to pursue, and then actively and creatively seek out ways to accomplish those goals. While her son works on his learning processes, Pamela works as a freelancer.

A former university-level academic and career adviser, in addition to being a journalist and working homeschooling parent, Pamela is an active writer. She has had a blog for many years, but with her recent book, she has transitioned into consulting with parents of homeschoolers. Developing a variety of product offerings including workshops, one-on-one consultations, as well as speaking and writing, Pamela has been incredibly successful facilitating her home life and her professional career.

In addition, one of the benefits of this process in Pamela's view is the ability to leverage both homeschooled-centered activities and the normal social process of her daily routine such that her son sees more than just a classroom during his formative years.

"We make the most of extracurricular activities offered in our community, especially those programs tailored to homeschooled families. I feel like our experience is pretty similar to what school kids get, but just not as many of them in the room. But they are sitting there 8 to 5 and we're out doing things. I feel like he's socialized for the world he's going to need to grow into and not just socialized for the school system."

For Pamela, and many other working parents, it is about personal choices and finding what works for each individual family. While she feels like right now homeschooling is the right choice for her son, she says she gets frustrated when she sees homeschoolers and teachers pitted against each other, as well as working parents and stay-at-home parents. "It's about parents having choices and being able to make the right choice for their individual child. I would love for every parent to have enough choices to make the right one for their child and not be limited."

There is a variety of different approaches to balance in work and life not just for freelancers but really for anyone. In this chapter, we have two examples of balancing work, home, and family. Each person's path was different, and while looking at examples can be helpful, the only person who can truly define what balance is right for you is you. And you can only do that by carefully considering your own priorities and then crafting your work processes around them.

17

Challenges and How to Overcome Them

Ask any independent professional about his or her biggest challenge and you will hear several common refrains. While getting set up and paying your taxes are tough and sometimes a pain, they are at least concrete challenges that can be solved by getting good advice from your trifecta of experts. However, beyond such practical matters as protecting yourself from lawsuits and avoiding tax penalties, some other issues are unique to the world of working independently.

Every profession and every job has its pros and cons. If you work for a company, you might have a boss you hate. You might have someone sitting in the cubicle next to you who has an annoying habit. The company could go out of business. You could lose your job. All of these things are risks to having a "normal" job. None of those is a risk to a freelancer.

When you are working independently, you are usually your own boss, so the risk of hating your boss is low. Not zero, we all have our days, but pretty low. And for those of us who choose to work in a space where other people are present, whether on a client's site, in a co-working space, or at a coffee shop, while you might have an annoying neighbor on a particular day, it is rare that you have to sit next to him or her 8 hours a day, 5 days a week. The risk of losing clients exists, but it is rare that you lose them all at once.

The problems that challenge independent professionals fall generally into three categories: too much work, not enough work, or problems with clients. Too much work doesn't seem like it would be much of an issue when you are first getting started, but once you get a few clients, you will find that each one takes a bit more time than what you are being paid for, which can suddenly make you feel like you are working far more than a

40-hour week. Add to that the time you have to spend to manage the business and suddenly you can be stretched to your limits. This is especially true because work tends to ebb and flow. Rather than having a steady and consistent stream of work, most freelancers oscillate between too much work and too little.

Too little work has its own issues. Sure, we all like to have a break now and then, but when no work means no money, those quiet times can be stressful. To be successful, it is important to set aside extra savings when times are busy to tide you over when things get slow. It is ideal if you can have three to six months of savings to buffer you from times when you don't have enough work, when you want to work on a side project, or when you just want to take a break. One of the best ways to build up a savings account is to put aside 20% of every check you receive for your rainy day fund. That, along with the 30% you are putting aside for taxes, does eat up a large percentage of your income, but if you build that discipline into your spending, you will be in good shape.

Within the context of too much work, too little work, and issues with clients, there are a few specific challenges that free agents face. They are no fun when they happen, but there are some strategies that you can use to navigate these rough patches successfully.

1. The dry spell
2. Burnout
3. Stretching yourself too thin
4. Bad clients
5. Scope creep

While I have experienced all of these myself, I have also talked to hundreds of free agents, and everyone agrees that these are not only the most common issues, but the ones that make people quit. So let's talk about each of them in turn, because knowing what to expect can help you make a plan to get through these tough issues.

THE DRY SPELL

First on the list of issues is the feast or famine nature of the workflow. It is a rare person who succeeds in maintaining a perfectly steady stream of work. Even the most consistent and devoted networker who has built up a strong personal brand occasionally has a dry spell—a period of time where, whatever the reason, the work just isn't there. Sometimes running low on work can be a welcome change if you have been working full-tilt for a few months. But a true dry spell happens when you finish not one but several projects and have a long stretch where you are really not making the money you want or need. So, how do you break out of a dry spell?

Network—The most common reason freelancers experience dry spells is because during a busy period, they stop having time to network. When you stop putting yourself out there, stop making those contacts day in and day out that lead to new work, the sales pipeline goes drier than the Sahara desert. To fill that pipeline with fresh business, you have to get back out there and start working your contacts. Go to meetings you haven't been to in a while. Join a co-working space and meet some new people. Volunteer. Whatever it takes, the first and best step you can take to get back into the game is to network.

Build a product—While many of us leverage our expertise on a dollar per hour basis, that strategy means that we only earn revenue when we are doing work. Having a product—something you can sell that doesn't require you to be physically there to deliver it—can help create a stream of income that is not directly dependent on you getting new clients. Create what? Well, that depends on what you do. The most common products that free agents produce are books (including e-books), apps, online courses and seminars, templates and tools, etc. It is easier than ever to create something using multi-media tools. So, if you have no client work, treat yourself like a client and build something you can sell.

Give a little away—A great way to generate leads is to give a little some-thing away. Package up an hour or two of your time into an assessment, a consultation, or some other freebie and then find a way to promote it for free. Auction sites like biddingforgood.com will take donations of time and goods to support a cause. Your local Chamber of Commerce can help you promote your freebie in its newsletters or through other channels. Partner up with someone that offers a service compatible with yours and offer a freebie to their clients.

Take a vacation—It may seem counterintuitive, especially if money is tight, but sometimes as an independent professional you have to take advantage of time when you have it. Feast or famine means sometimes you have more work than you can handle, and while you might be rak-ing in the cash during those times, it can lead to burnout. So if you have a chance to take a break, take a real break. Don't spend the whole time fretting about your lack of business development—take a full week off and do something entirely different. Taking time for yourself can re-energize you and when you get back, you will have a new perspective on everything, which often leads to new opportunities for work.

BURNOUT

While dry spells can be deadly for your confidence as well as your cash flow, their polar opposite can sometimes be even worse. Burnout happens when you are working too much or working on the wrong things. For many free agents who are just starting out, any work is good work. However, spending too much time on projects you don't really like will drain your energy, leaving you no time or inclination to pursue the work you do like. Battling burnout can be tough because often it sneaks up on you. You think everything is fine, but then you snap at your kids when they ask you when you are going to be done on the computer. You find yourself procrastinating simple things because you just don't feel like doing any of the things that are on your plate.

Burnout is subtle and insidious—it creeps into your workday and sucks out all the joy and fun you used to find in having a flexible schedule and being able to choose the work you like. Climbing back up out of burnout can be hard, too, especially if you don't have enough of the right work to pay the bills. However, there are some ways you can battle burnout and get back to a better relationship with your clients and your career path.

Talk to a colleague—It is easy to feel isolated as a freelancer. We all have times when we feel sunk down into our own worlds. As part of the sales process and the client management process, as we talked about in Chapter 12, part of a consultant's job is to put a good face on things and never complain to a client. However, not complaining to a client is different from not seeking out support when you need it. You should have a network of supportive colleagues who you can go to when you are struggling. While it is tempting to go to your friends, if they aren't self-employed, they probably won't be able to help. The very best people to talk to are other free agents who can offer you support and advice.

Make some referrals—If the problem is that you have filled your calendar with work you can do but don't love, it is time to refer some of that work to other freelancers. Pick your least favorite two clients and either wrap up your projects with them if you can, or subcontract them to people you know who love to do that work. Here is an example. I started my career in IT support, and I still often am asked to do technology assessment or tactical technology integration work. If I have a gap in my schedule, and I want to help the person who is asking, I might say yes. Ultimately, it is not work that I love to do and if I fill my schedule with those types of engagements, I won't be very happy. I do know quite a few people who do that work and do it really well. Therefore, I try to be disciplined about making referrals when that work comes up. In turn, I often get referrals from my colleagues who do IT consulting but don't like it when the engagement is truly about operations and change management.

Getting to know people who do things that are close to what you do or even that overlap is a good thing. It means that you can share the load when there is too much work to be done, and you can ask for referrals when things are slow.

STRETCHING YOURSELF TOO THIN

Another type of burnout happens when you stretch yourself too thin. This is different than taking too much work; in fact, it often happens when you don't have enough work and decide to save money by running some of the operational aspects of your business yourself.

It is hard enough to juggle all of the things involved in working independently when times are good. Between doing sales and marketing, service delivery, finance, and accounting as well as chief cook and bottle washer, it seems like there is never enough time. If you are making enough money to do it, the very first thing you can and should do is outsource some of the day-to-day work, especially if it is not your strength. However, what do you do when there is not enough money to go around?

Barter—If you haven't been making enough to pay someone to help out with your IT, your billing, or your website management, it is time to think about the barter system. While not everyone will be willing to trade help for help, some will and this can be a big cost savings. I help some of my freelance friends get their email set up and give them advice on technology issues. In return, I get help with marketing and branding. Always ask if someone is open to bartering before you assume he or she is willing, but otherwise bartering can be a good way to extend your own capacity.

Use technology—Technology doesn't solve every problem, but it can definitely help you stay organized and communicate better. Tools like the VIP inbox on Apple devices and email flags in Outlook can help ensure you don't miss important emails when you are running around. Calendaring tools can keep you on track when you are on the road, and task management systems like ToDo and Asana are great ways to keep it all together. Some days it can seem like there are 100 tools for every task, and even the idea of sitting down and choosing the right technology to keep you up to date can be overwhelming. But it is well worth a little time investment to set yourself up so that bills are paid, invoices are sent out, and your calendar goes with you wherever you go.

BAD CLIENTS

Besides struggling with time and motivation, sometimes the biggest challenges come from clients. It won't take very many gigs for you to find at least one client who pushes the envelope in terms of professional behavior. Sometimes it is calling too early or too late at night. Other times it is micromanagement. There is a wide variety of ways that clients can make your life difficult. However, isn't the customer always right? Not always.

Clients can behave badly in all kinds of different ways, but ultimately there are only a few strategies you can use to deal with client issues, no matter how they manifest themselves.

Walk away—This is the most drastic option, and usually it is last on the list of alternatives. However, it is an important tool and sometimes it is the right choice. If a client is verbally abusive (yes, this happens) or makes you feel uncomfortable, it is time to seriously consider pulling the plug on the engagement. If a client doesn't pay but wants you to keep right on working, it is time to think about walking away. With no HR department to report issues to, and your own time and money at risk, you need to be your own advocate if you feel like a client has crossed over the boundary of reasonable professional behavior.

Set boundaries—When you first start to feel like an engagement is getting off track, that is the time to have a conversation with your client before things get out of hand. Call it a check-in and schedule a meeting to talk about progress. Discuss what has happened and what is still in progress. Then ask your clients if there is any feedback they would like to give you at this point. If they have feedback to offer, that is great. Then you can offer feedback of your own. Sometimes you will be working with someone who has not managed a contractor before, and he or she may not have read or understood the scope of work.

SCOPE CREEP

One very specific type of client issue that comes up frequently is scope creep. We talked about this first back in Chapter 7 when we looked at the structure of proposals and contracts. Ideally, if you have a well-written scope, it can be a good tool to return to if your client is asking for things that are outside the boundaries of what you agreed to do. Remember that scope creep is an opportunity to get more business out of a client, but only if you address the issue up front, and let the client know that if it wants that extra work done, the client is going to need to add to the time and cost of the project.

This is where a change of scope form is a great tool. When a client starts asking you to do things that were not part of the original agreement, you can respond that you would be happy to do that work (or find a contractor to help you get it done) and that you will send over a change of scope to include this new deliverable. A change of scope form articulates the time and cost of the new work, and clearly shows that this is outside the bounds of the original project. If the client signs, all is well and you just gained more hours. If the client balks, you simply fall back to the original scope, and you have made your point that you won't be including that extra work.

Client communication is a fine line to walk. On the one hand, you want to be accommodating and helpful. On the other hand, you can't be trapped into doing far more work than you bargained for without getting paid for it.

While there are many great benefits to being a free agent, it certainly comes with its fair share of challenges too. Burnout, stretching yourself too thin, having dry spells, and having a tough time with your clients are things that happen to us all. The very best thing you can do to sustain yourself through the tough times is to cultivate a strong network of other independent professionals that you can lean on when times are hard. Sometimes you just need to vent about a tough day or a project that is going poorly. Having a great network can be the glue that helps you hold it all together for the long haul.

18

References and Notes

INTRODUCTION

MBO Partners 2013 State of Independence in America Third Annual Independent Workforce Report: http://info.mbopartners.com/rs/mbo/images/2013-MBO_Partners_State_of_Independence_Report.pdf

GAO 2006 Employment Arrangement Report: http://www.gao.gov/new.items/d06656.pdf

Conference Board Job Satisfaction 2013 Report: https://www.conference-board.org/publications/publicationdetail.cfm?publicationid=2522

Gallup State of the Global Workforce Report: http://www.gallup.com/strategicconsulting/164735/state-global-workplace.aspx

ElanceFreelanceTalentReport2011:https://www.elance.com/q/freelance-talent-report-2011

CHAPTER 1

Herman Miller company history: http://www.hermanmiller.com/content/hermanmiller/northamerica/en_us/home/about-us/who-is-herman-miller/company-timeline/1900.html

D.J. DePree Obituary and Biography: http://www.nytimes.com/1990/12/13/obituaries/d-j-depree-who-broke-ground-in-furniture-design-is-dead-at-99.html

Herman Miller 2013 Workplace Trends Survey: https://www.hermanmiller.com/content/dam/hermanmiller/documents/research_topics/2013_Workplace_Trends.pdf

Revenue Act of 1978 and its impact on pension plans: http://www.ebri.org/pdf/publications/facts/1298fact.pdf

Section 530: Its History and Application in Light of the Federal Definition of the Employer-Employee Relationship for Federal Tax Purposes: http://www.irs.gov/pub/irs-utl/irpac-br_530_relief_-_appendix_natrm_paper_09032009.pdf

Towers Watson study on pension plans in Fortune 100 companies: http://www.towerswatson.com/en-US/Insights/Newsletters/Americas/insider/2012/retirement-plan-type-of-fortune-100-companies-in-2012

Henry S. Farber, Employment Insecurity: The Decline in Worker-Firm Attachment in the United States, Princeton University research study on employee tenure changes since 1975: http://www.princeton.edu/ceps/workingpapers/172farber.pdf

Timothy Ferris, *The Four Hour Workweek*, Harmony, 2009.

Intuit 2020 Small Business Report: http://http-download.intuit.com/http.intuit/CMO/intuit/futureofsmallbusiness/intuit_2020_report.pdf

Chris Brogan, Human Business Works: http://www.humanbusinessworks.com, http://www.chrisbrogan.com

CHAPTER 2

Labor Market Data, September 2014, U.S. Bureau of Labor Statistics: http://www.bls.gov/web/empsit/cps_charts.pdf

Commuting in the U.S., 2009, U.S. Census: http://www.census.gov/prod/2011pubs/acs-15.pdf

Home Based Workers, 2010, U.S. Census: http://www.census.gov/hhes/commuting/files/2012/Home-based%20Workers%20in%20the%20United%20States-Paper.pdf

Bright Horizons Modern Family Index 2014: http://www.brighthorizons.com/about-us/press-releases/working-parents-fear-family-responsibilities-could-cost-their-job/

Stephen Sweet and Jacquelyn B. James, "What do Managers Really Think about Flexibility?" The Sloan Center on Aging and Work at Boston College: http://www.bc.edu/content/dam/files/research_sites/agingandwork/pdf/publications/IB26_TPM.pdf

Work Market: http://www.workmarket.com

Affordable Care Act Full-Time Employee Definitions: http://www.irs.gov/pub/irs-drop/n-12-58.pdf

Recession of 2007-2009, U.S. Bureau of Labor Statistics: http://www.bls.gov/spotlight/2012/recession/pdf/recession_bls_spotlight.pdf

Nathaniel Kleitman, *Sleep and Wakefulness*, University of Chicago Press, 1987.

Peretz Lavie, Ultradian Rhythms in Prolonged Human Performance: http://www.ntis.gov/search/product.aspx?ABBR=ADA296199

Susan Cain, *Quiet: The Power of Introverts in a World that Can't Stop Talking*, Broadway Books, 2013.

CHAPTER 3

Peter Shankman: http://www.shankman.com

Steve Woodruff: http://www.stevewoodruff.com

CHAPTER 4

Tammy Strobel, *You Can Buy Happiness (And It's Cheap)*, New World Library, 2012: www.tammystrobel.com

American Psychiatric Association, Hoarding Disorder, http://www.psychiatry.org/hoarding-disorder

Consumer Credit Outstanding, U.S. Federal Reserve: http://www.federalreserve.gov/releases/g19/hist/cc_hist_sa_levels.html

Tumbleweed Tiny Houses: http://www.tumbleweedhouses.com

PAD (Portland Alternative Dwellings): http://padtinyhouses.com/

Greywater Action information on composting toilets: http://greywateraction.org/content/about-composting-toilets

Tiny House Talk: http://www.tinyhousetalk.com

CHAPTER 5

Strange Brewing trademark dispute: http://blogs.denverpost.com/beer/2014/03/21/trademark-dispute-strange-craft-beer-company-born/13331/, http://blogs.westword.com/cafesociety/2012/11/strange_brewing_trademark_threat.php

Cornell University Law School definition of piercing the veil: http://www.law.cornell.edu/wex/piercing_the_corporate_veil

American Bar Association lawyer referral directory: http://apps.americanbar.org/legalservices/lris/directory/

U.S. Chamber of Commerce Institute for Legal Reform: Lawsuit Climate Report, 2012: http://www.instituteforlegalreform.com/uploads/sites/1/Lawsuit_Climate_Report_2012.pdf

CHAPTER 6

National Association of State Boards of Accountancy (NASBA): http://nasba.org

IRS standard mileage rates: http://www.irs.gov/Tax-Professionals/Standard-Mileage-Rates

Intuit: http://www.intuit.com

Mint: http://www.mint.com

Freshbooks: http://www.freshbooks.com

CHAPTER 7

IRS Small Business and Self-Employed Tax Center: http://www.irs.gov/Businesses/Small-Businesses-&-Self-Employed/Small-Business-and-Self-Employed-Tax-Center-1

IRS Business Expenses Publication 535: http://www.irs.gov/pub/irs-pdf/p535.pdf

Electronic Federal Tax Payment System (EFTPS): https://www.eftps.gov/eftps/

CHAPTER 8

National Geographic statistics on probability of being struck by lightning: http://news. nationalgeographic.com/news/2004/06/0623_040623_lightningfacts.html

National Fire Protection Association (NFPA) statistics on fire losses in the U.S.: http:// www.nfpa.org/research/reports-and-statistics/fires-in-the-us/overall-fire-problem/ fire-loss-in-the-united-states

Social Security Administration (SSA) probability of being disabled: http://www.ssa.gov/ pressoffice/basicfact.htm

CHAPTER 9

International Freelance Academy 2012 Industry Report: http://www.internationalfreelanc-ersday.com/2012report/

CHAPTER 10

Youth Entrepreneurship Study by Buzz Marketing Group and Young Entrepreneurs Council, 2011: http://www.slideshare.net/twfashion/yecbuzz-marketing-group-youth-entrepreneurship-study

http://www.buzzmg.com

http://www.youngentrepreneurcouncil.com

Freelancing in America: A National Survey of the New Workforce: Freelancers Union and Elance-oDesk, 2014: http://fu-web-storage-prod.s3.amazonaws.com/content/filer_ public/c2/06/c2065a8a-7f00-46db-915a-2122965df7d9/fu_freelancinginamericare-port_v3-rgb.pdf

CHAPTER 11

Amanda Palmer, The Art of Asking: http://www.ted.com/talks/amanda_palmer _the_art_of_asking

Adam Grant, *Give and Take*, Penguin, 2013.

CHAPTER 12

Deion Sanders Biography: http://www.deion-sanders.com/bio.html
Abraham Maslow Biography: http://webspace.ship.edu/cgboer/maslow.html
Katie Probert: http://jesuisunemonstre.blogspot.com/
Edventure Project: http://www.edventureproject.com

CHAPTER 13

Workbar: http://www.workbar.com
Deskmag Global Co-working Survey: http://www.slideshare.net/deskwanted/global-coworking-survey-2012?ref=http://blog.deskwanted.com/, http://www.deskmag.com/en/the-coworking-market-report-forecast-2014
Bernard DeKoven and the co-working connection: http://www.deepfun.com/fun/2013/08/the-coworking-connection/
History of Co-working: http://www.tiki-toki.com/timeline/entry/156192/The-History-Of-Coworking-Presented-By-Deskmag#vars!date=1996-06-11_06:17:29!
Elance Global Online Employment Report: https://www.elance.com/q/online-employment-report
Millenials and the Future of Work Study by Elance-oDesk: https://www.odesk.com/info/spring2013onlineworksurvey/
Intuit 2020 Trend Report: http://http-download.intuit.com/http.intuit/CMO/intuit/future-ofsmallbusiness/intuit_2020_report.pdf
General Assembly: http://www.generalassembly.com

CHAPTER 14

Mike Markkula Biography: http://www.biography.com/people/mike-markkula-21187327
Walter Isaacson, *Steve Jobs*, Simon & Schuster, 2011.
ReferenceUSA: www.referenceUSA.com

CHAPTER 15

David Maister, Charles H. Green, and Robert M. Galford, *The Trusted Advisor*, Free Press, 2001.

CHAPTER 16

Penelope Trunk: http://www.penelopetrunk.com

American Express survey: http://about.americanexpress.com/news/pr/2012/sst.aspx

Nicholas Carr, *The Shallows: What the Internet is Doing to Our Brains*, W.W. Norton & Company, 2011.

Sherry Turkle, *Alone Together: Why We Expect More from Technology and Less from Each Other*, Basic Books, 2011.

National Center for Education Statistics: http://nces.ed.gov/fastfacts/display.asp?id=91

Pamela Price: http://www.pamelaprice.com

Pamela Price, *How to Work and Homeschool*, GHF Press, 2013.

CHAPTER 17

Bidding for Good: http://www.biddingforgood.com

Appendix

U.S. companies are regulated by each individual state. In this appendix, you will find links to each state's website, which includes forms and information about how to form and operate a corporation in that state. Because your business name will need to be unique within the state, you can also search by business entity name to make sure the name you choose doesn't overlap with someone else.

In addition to searching within your state, it is also a good idea to search the U.S. Patent and Trademark Office database to make sure your business name is not already registered by someone else. That database is here:

http://www.uspto.gov/trademarks/index.jsp

Alabama

Incorporation Forms and Information: http://www.sos.state.al.us/BusinessServices/Default.aspx

Business Name Search: http://arc-sos.state.al.us/CGI/CORPNAME.MBR/INPUT

Alaska

Incorporation Forms and Information: http://commerce.state.ak.us/dnn/cbpl/BusinessLicensing.aspx

Business Name Search: http://commerce.alaska.gov/CBP/Main/CBPLSearch.aspx?mode=Corp

Arizona

Incorporation Forms and Information: http://www.azcc.gov/divisions/corporations/

Business Name Search: http://www.azsos.gov/scripts/TNT_Search_engine.dll

Arkansas

Incorporation Forms and Information: http://www.sos.arkansas.gov/
BCS/Pages/default.aspx

Business Name Search: http://www.sos.arkansas.gov/corps/search_all.
php

California

Incorporation Forms and Information: http://www.sos.ca.gov/busi-
ness/be/forms.htm

Business Name Search: http://kepler.sos.ca.gov/

Colorado

Incorporation Forms and Information: http://www.sos.state.co.us/
pubs/business/businessHome.html?menuheaders=2

Business Name Search: http://www.sos.state.co.us/biz/BusinessEntity
CriteriaExt.do

Connecticut

Incorporation Forms and Information: http://www.ct.gov/sots/site/default.
asp

Business Name Search: http://www.concord-sots.ct.gov/CONCORD/
online?sn=PublicInquiry&eid=9740

Delaware

Incorporation Forms and Information: http://www.corp.delaware.gov/
howtoform.shtml

Business Name Search: https://delecorp.delaware.gov/tin/GIName
Search.jsp

District of Columbia

Incorporation Forms and Information: http://dmped.dc.gov/page/
start-business

Business Name Search: https://corp.dcra.dc.gov/Account.aspx/LogOn?
ReturnUrl=%2fHome.aspx

Florida

Incorporation Forms and Information: http://sunbiz.org/startbus.html

Business Name Search: http://search.sunbiz.org/Inquiry/Corporation Search/ByName

Georgia

Incorporation Forms and Information: http://sos.georgia.gov/corporations/

Business Name Search: https://cgov.sos.state.ga.us/Account.aspx/LogOn?ReturnUrl=%2f

Hawaii

Incorporation Forms and Information: http://hawaii.gov/dcca/areas/breg/registration/

Business Name Search: https://hbe.ehawaii.gov/documents/search.html?mobile=N&site_preference=normal

Idaho

Incorporation Forms and Information: http://www.sos.idaho.gov/CORP/reservation.htm

Business Name Search: http://www.accessidaho.org/public/sos/corp/search.html?ScriptForm.startstep=crit

Illinois

Incorporation Forms and Information: http://business.illinois.gov/registration.cfm

Business Name Search: http://www.cyberdriveillinois.com/departments/business_services/corp.html

Indiana

Incorporation Forms and Information: http://www.in.gov/sos/business/index.htm

Business Name Search: https://secure.in.gov/sos/online_corps/name_search.aspx

Iowa

Incorporation Forms and Information: http://sos.iowa.gov/business/FormsAndFees.html

Business Name Search: https://sos.iowa.gov/search/business/%28S%284yqwafvuaeh1rq3ki44l0xec%29%29/search.aspx

Kansas

Incorporation Forms and Information: http://www.kssos.org/forms/forms_results.asp?division=BS

Business Name Search: https://www.kansas.gov/bess/flow/main?execution=e1s2

Kentucky

Incorporation Forms and Information: http://sos.ky.gov/business/filings/

Business Name Search: https://app.sos.ky.gov/ftsearch/?path=nameavail

Louisiana

Incorporation Forms and Information: http://www.sos.louisiana.gov/tabid/97/Default.aspx

Business Name Search: http://www.sos.la.gov/BusinessServices/SearchForLouisianaBusinessFilings/Pages/default.aspx

Maine

Incorporation Forms and Information: http://www.maine.gov/portal/business/corporate.html

Business Name Search: https://icrs.informe.org/nei-sos-icrs/ICRS?MainPage=x

Maryland

Incorporation Forms and Information: http://www.dat.state.md.us/sdatweb/sdatforms.html

Business Name Search: http://sdatcert3.resiusa.org/ucc-charter/Pages/CharterSearch/default.aspx

Massachusetts

Incorporation Forms and Information: http://www.sec.state.ma.us/cor/coridx.htm

Business Name Search: http://corp.sec.state.ma.us/CorpWeb/Name Reservation/SearchNameRes.aspx

Michigan

Incorporation Forms and Information: https://www.michigan.gov/lara/0,4601,7-154-35299_61343_35413_36736—-,00.html

Business Name Search: http://www2.dleg.state.mi.us/CORPORATIONS/htmldb/f?p=210:1:6772285934866496

Minnesota

Incorporation Forms and Information: http://www.sos.state.mn.us/index.aspx?page=331

Business Name Search: http://mblsportal.sos.state.mn.us/

Mississippi

Incorporation Forms and Information: http://www.sos.ms.gov/business_services_business_formation.aspx

Business Name Search: http://business.sos.ms.gov/star/portal/msbsd/page/uccSearch-stand/portal.aspx

Missouri

Incorporation Forms and Information: http://www.sos.mo.gov/business/corporations/

Business Name Search: https://bsd.sos.mo.gov/BusinessEntity/BESearch.aspx?SearchType=0

Montana

Incorporation Forms and Information: http://www.sos.mt.gov/Business/Forms/index.asp

Business Name Search: https://app.mt.gov/bes/

Nebraska

Incorporation Forms and Information: http://www.sos.ne.gov/business/corp_serv/index.html

Business Name Search: https://www.nebraska.gov/sos/corp/corpsearch.cgi#searchform

Nevada

Incorporation Forms and Information: https://www.nvsilverflume.gov/startBusiness

Business Name Search: https://www.nvsilverflume.gov/businessSearch

New Hampshire

Incorporation Forms and Information: http://www.sos.nh.gov/corporate/

Business Name Search: https://www.sos.nh.gov/corporate/soskb/csearch.asp

New Jersey

Incorporation Forms and Information: http://www.nj.gov/njbusiness/

Business Name Search: https://www.njportal.com/DOR/BusinessNameSearch/default.aspx

New Mexico

Incorporation Forms and Information: http://www.nmprc.state.nm.us/index.html

Business Name Search: https://portal.sos.state.nm.us/corps/%28S%28qxzgldcb43e3w54txuuyurqd%29%29/Corplookup/Lookdn.aspx

New York

Incorporation Forms and Information: http://www.dos.ny.gov/corps/

Business Name Search: http://www.dos.ny.gov/corps/bus_entity_search.html

North Carolina

Incorporation Forms and Information: http://www.secretary.state. nc.us/Corporations/

Business Name Search: http://www.secretary.state.nc.us/corporations/ csearch.aspx

North Dakota

Incorporation Forms and Information: http://www.nd.gov/sos/businessserv/registrations/index.html

Business Name Search: https://apps.nd.gov/sc/busnsrch/busnSearch. htm

Ohio

Incorporation Forms and Information: http://www.sos.state.oh.us/ SOS/Businesses.aspx

Business Name Search: http://www2.sos.state.oh.us/pls/bsqry/f?p= 100:1:0:::::

Oklahoma

Incorporation Forms and Information: https://www.sos.ok.gov/business/forms.aspx

Business Name Search: https://www.sos.ok.gov/corp/corpinquiryfind. aspx

Oregon

Incorporation Forms and Information: http://sos.oregon.gov/business/ Pages/default.aspx

Business Name Search: http://egov.sos.state.or.us/br/pkg_web_name_ srch_inq.login

Pennsylvania

Incorporation Forms and Information: https://www.corporations.state. pa.us/corp/soskb/csearch.asp

Business Name Search: https://www.corporations.state.pa.us/corp/ soskb/csearch.asp

Rhode Island

Incorporation Forms and Information: http://sos.ri.gov/business/
Business Name Search: http://ucc.state.ri.us/CorpSearch/CorpSearch
Input.asp

South Carolina

Incorporation Forms and Information: http://www.sos.sc.gov/
Business_Filings
Business Name Search: http://www.scsos.com/Search%20Business%20
Filings

South Dakota

Incorporation Forms and Information: http://www.sdsos.gov/busine-
services/corporations.shtm
Business Name Search: https://sos.sd.gov/business/search.aspx

Tennessee

Incorporation Forms and Information: http://www.state.tn.us/#business
Business Name Search: https://tnbear.tn.gov/ecommerce/nameavail-
ability.aspx

Texas

Incorporation Forms and Information: http://www.sos.state.tx.us/corp/
forms_option.shtml
Business Name Search: http://www.sos.state.tx.us/corp/sosda/index.
shtml

Utah

Incorporation Forms and Information: http://www.corporations.utah.
gov/index.html
Business Name Search: https://secure.utah.gov/bes/

Vermont

Incorporation Forms and Information: https://www.sec.state.vt.us/corporations.aspx
Business Name Search: https://www.vtsosonline.com/online/BusinessInquire/

Virginia

Incorporation Forms and Information: http://www.scc.virginia.gov/clk/begin.aspx
Business Name Search: https://sccefile.scc.virginia.gov/Find/Business

Washington

Incorporation Forms and Information: http://www.secstate.wa.gov/corps/
Business Name Search: http://www.sos.wa.gov/corps/corps_search.aspx

West Virginia

Incorporation Forms and Information: http://www.sos.wv.gov/business-licensing/Pages/default.aspx
Business Name Search: http://apps.sos.wv.gov/business/corporations/

Wisconsin

Incorporation Forms and Information: http://www.wdfi.org/corporations/
Business Name Search: https://www.wdfi.org/apps/CorpSearch/Search.aspx

Wyoming

Incorporation Forms and Information: http://soswy.state.wy.us/Business/Default.aspx
Business Name Search: https://wyobiz.wy.gov/business/filingsearch.aspx

Index

About the Author

Katy Tynan is a free agent. Working where people and technology come together, she provides strategy and operational guidance to high-growth organizations. Katy is currently engaged in a variety of activities including consulting, writing, and speaking. She is passionate about how the world of work is changing, and how individuals, businesses, and educational institutions need to adapt to the evolving landscape of flexible work.

Prior to her transition to being a full-time independent professional, Katy was part of the leadership teams of several successful startups including Thrive Networks (acquired by Staples) and Winphoria Networks (acquired by Motorola).

When she is not helping solve business and technology problems, Katy can be found traveling, kayaking, sailing, or reading. Katy, her son, and her dog live near Boston, Massachusetts, and she is a proud graduate of UMass Amherst.